M000295280

DIVINE MESSAGES FOR HUMANITY

Channeled Communication from the Other Side on Death, the Afterlife, the Ego, Prejudices, Prayer and the Power of Love

KEVIN HUNTER

Warrior of Light Press

www.kevin-hunter.com

Body, Mind & Spirit/Angels & Guides
Inspiration & Personal Growth

PRODUCTION CREDITS:

Project Editor: James Szopo

Author back cover photo by photographer, Edwin Santiago
www.edwinsantiago.com

Acknowledgements

Thank you to my spiritual posse that consists of God and my personal sports team of Angels, Guides, Archangels and Saints. I would also like to thank Saint Nathaniel and his team of disciples on the other side for giving me the majority of the information contained in this book.

Chapters

Warrior of Light
book series

Spirit Guides and Angels: How I Communicate with Heaven

Soul Mates and Twin Flames: Attracting in Love, Friendships and the Human Heart

Divine Messages for Humanity: Channeled Communication from the Other Side on Death, the Afterlife, the Ego, Prejudices, Prayer and the Power of Love

Raising Your Vibration: Fine Tune Your Body & Soul to Receive Messages from Heaven

Connecting with the Archangels

Author's Note

This book is part of a series of *Warrior of Light* books. Some of the content in all of the books are available in a greatest hits book called, *Warrior of Light: Messages from my Guides and Angels.*

All of the *Warrior of Light* books are infused with practical messages and guidance that my Spirit team has taught and shared with me revolving around many different topics. The main goal is to fine tune your soul, which subsequently improves humanity at the same time. You are a Divine communicator and perfectly adjusted and capable of receiving messages from Heaven. This is for your benefit in order to live a happier, richer life. It is your individual responsibility to respect yourself and this planet while on your journey here.

The messages and information enclosed in this and in all of the *Warrior of Light* books may be in my own words, but they do not come from me. They come from God, the Holy Spirit, my Spirit team of guides, angels and sometimes certain Archangels and Saints. I am merely the liaison or messenger in delivering and interpreting the intentions of what they wish to communicate. They love that I talk about them and share this stuff as it gets other people to work with them too!

There is one main hierarchy Saint who works with me leading the pack. His name is Nathaniel. He can be brutally truthful and forceful, as he does not mince words. There may be topics in this and the other books that might bother you or make you uncomfortable. He asks that you examine the underlying cause of this discomfort and come to terms with the fear that is attached to it. He cuts right to the heart of humanity without apology. I have learned quite a bit from him while adopting his ideology, which is Heaven's as a whole.

I am one with the Holy Spirit and have many Spirit Guides and Angels around me. As my connections to the other side grew to be daily over the course of my life, more of them joined in behind the others. I have seen, sensed, heard and been privy to the dozens of magnificent lights that crowd around me on occasion.

If I use the word "He" when pertaining to God, this does not mean that I am advocating that he is a male. Simply replace the word, "He" with one you are comfortable using to identify God for you to be. This goes for any gender I use as examples. When I say, "spirit team", I am referring to a team of 'Guides and Angels'. The purpose of the *Warrior of Light* books are to empower you and help you to improve yourself, your life and humanity as a whole. It does not matter if you are a beginner or well versed in the subject matter. There may be something in these books that reminds you of something you already know or something that you were unaware of. We all have much to share with one another, as we are all one in the end. This book and all of the *Warrior of Light* series of books contain information and directions on how to reach the place where you can be a fine tuned instrument to receive your own messages from your own Spirit team.

Some of my personal stories are infused in the books in order for you to live vicariously through osmosis on how it works effectively for me. With some of my methods I hope that you gain insight, knowledge or inspiration out of it. It may prompt you to recall incidents where you were receiving divine messages in your own life. There are helpful ways that you can improve your existence and have a connection with Heaven throughout these books. Doing so will greatly transform yourself in all ways allowing you to attract wonderful circumstances at higher levels and live a happier more content life.

~ Kevin Hunter

DIVINE MESSAGES FOR HUMANITY

Chapter One

HELL AND THE DEVIL: THE REAL MONSTERS OF SOCIETY. THE EGO.

$\mathcal{I}$ receive many questions and inquiries about all sorts of things from dating and relationship advice to what happens when we die. In this book are some of the things that my Spirit team of Guides and Angels have shared with me throughout my life. This particular chapter contains words that my spearheading hierarchy guide, Saint Nathaniel, has relayed to me with his team of disciples who reside in another dimension in the spirit world. He has played an integral part in contributing the tough love messages I voice that essentially come from God. He is someone who does not mince words as I state from time to time. He has even scolded me the way a stern Father might. It is not cruel and abusive, but firm and out of love. I have interpreted and worded the messages as best I can, even though pronouns may be confusing at times. You should still be able to grasp the concept and the ultimate message.

Saint Nathaniel's message
interpreted by the author:

Prejudices towards other people who are different from you have been going on for centuries. Someone's skin color is a different shade, or their features appear much different than yours, or they have a different religion, or sexual orientation than you, or your community and they are lambasted, criticized, attacked and at times killed! You would think that after all these years on Earth and the progression of civilization that you would have learned something while you have been here. Instead you allow other people and their surroundings to easily influence you causing one to form a false reality. You were all placed here to teach, learn, experience and give love. Why has this most easy and wonderfully uplifting task been so magnificently difficult for some of you? You are all here for this reason. Working on those attributes accelerates your soul's growth.

You have been given a body as a protective shell to function while on Earth. Your Spirit soul is your true self and who you are at the core. Your body is a vessel you are renting for a short amount of time in order to live and function in the Earth's dense atmosphere. You came into this world for a purpose and it is your goal to find out what that is and master it. It can be something as simple as learning to forgive others or to control your anger. You must discover this purpose on your own.

Your body is not meant to last eternally, but your soul is. Your bodies were designed to age over a period of time. There is no avoiding this. You can have all the plastic surgery you want in an attempt to keep your outer appearance appearing young. This will not stop the process internally. Your health and organs that keep your soul alive in your body will eventually falter, fail or stop working. This is nothing to be afraid of. The sooner you realize this, then the quicker and easier your transition will be into the spirit world or whatever labels you associate Heaven to be for you.

The average Earthly existence is a day long in comparison to life in the next world. When you pass on to the next life, your body is left to disintegrate on Earth and is no longer needed as you move on to paradise. This presents many challenges for those in this lifetime. The Ego has become a wild and unruly monster crippling millions of human souls. You force feed negative images and stories to one another on a daily basis off of the internet alone which you have created. This ranges from salacious gossip sites to antagonistic news sites and sources that only feature the worst press worthy information provided specifically to control your Ego. They blow it up and sensationalize it. The planet and its people are hypnotized succumbing to its allure. They take pieces of this behavior and incorporate it into their personalities. They then impose it onto friends, family and communities who do the same to others. Suddenly you have this wave of negativity and gossip that has taken over the planet. This energy magnetizes it back to one another ten fold causing a flurry of anger and toxicity that plagues your bodies, souls and your surroundings.

You go to the comment boards on the Internet or wherever those who have too much time on their hands frequent and you find criticisms and negative statements about someone else. The destructive tendencies of the human Ego are alive and well. This was not what we intended for your soul. You did not agree to this when you chose to live an Earthly life. You forgot who you are my child. We do not say any of this to punish or judge you. The only judging that takes place is the one you produce.

You take everything personally and react negatively mirroring it back to one another. Soon you have a minefield of bickering and snide energy that is unleashed on the Internet and social media alone. This is transported into the heavens and reflected back to all of you tenfold. Some of you do this callously and naively. In this state you are emulating your lower selves. Many of you are not learning from your mistakes, and nor are you aware of how you treat others, while some of you do not care at all. You are lost in a field of ugliness that you perpetuate daily. You feed off of it and on each other's Egos to one up the next person and make sure your opinion is the one that is gold.

There was a story in the news about a brave fourteen-year-old girl activist from Pakistan. She posted a blog about women having the right to an education. She continued on her crusade despite threats from the Taliban. As a result, the Taliban stopped the school bus she was on and shot her in the head and neck leaving her in critical condition. This is the difference between a girl with no choice and one in America who has several choices.

The media and their peers are leading the youth of today. They are more interested in attracting sex or looking desirable than fixing this world. Still – they are more spiritually inclined than any of the previous generations. They have been chosen to bring peace and love into this world as long as they do not follow the path of the Ego.

Some religions preach about a Hell and a Devil. The real Hell is on Earth and the Devil resides in all of you and has been unleashed with great magnitude. The impact is greater than the largest tidal wave, earthquake or meteor rock to ever threaten to smash into Earth. Those who stand in front of a pulpit to deliver fiery sermons are not protected or exempt from this. They are given a platform to reach many responsibly and are not encouraged to misuse that position as some do. Young people pose provocatively online. They are naive and heavily influenced by the mirage of the internets fictitious attention. The photos show where their self-esteem is at which is not in a good place to begin with. This is what some of you feel the need to do to receive instant validation, which is not true confirmation at all. They learn this message from their parents, peers, communities and media. It is a vicious cycle of mythology that has no truth. Your beauty shines through regardless of provocative poses. Many of you tend to put up these photos for various reasons. Sometimes it is just for fun and other times it is an attempt to feel validated and loved. This opens up a bigger can of worms and another plethora of issues that need to be addressed in the world by your media.

There is a rush that some of you get from what seems like positive attention. It is not positive attention as it is false devotion. You are not being loved for who you are, but how you look and what you have. The last two are products of the Ego when in truth you were born with God's holy light regardless of your belief systems. You have discovered that when you post hyper-sexualized photos that you receive more attention. No one is paying attention to you or your true soul dear one. You are blinded by what is not real. Nothing you can do can take away God's love for you. These are good children who are misguided. It prompts them to get love through unhealthy sources that only lower their self-esteem. It makes us sad to see people agonize and suffer for attention that is all a hallucination to begin with. Who you are in spirit and what you set out to do is who you truly are. How you treat others and the love and compassion that you display for others is why you are here. Stay away from gossip, negativity, hate or institutions that persecute others. You are all to be a role model of peace and love allowing God's light to shine within and around you.

When you pass on to the other side, your bodies are left behind and your soul is in tact and healthy in all ways again. What we in spirit see is a glow around us and around you. This glow has a varying brightness depending on one's spiritual evolvement and growth on Earth. On the other side, it is your glow that is looked upon with the love and attraction you crave. On Earth you are attracted to the physical look of the body your soul was born into. This attraction is removed as the body ages and dies. Your soul then becomes a light and that light is the main attraction to other souls. If you are inclined to be an attractive soul, then focus inward and work on your spiritual growth and become who you truly are and always have been. Look within and ignore the rest of it around you.

A dark fog layer has been created around the Earth's atmosphere. This is due to things like the high amount of toxins that human souls consume into their bodies feeding their emotional states and with the venom they emit at each other. This is a layer of thick smog particles that appear as heavy tar. It separates the Earth plane from the Spirit plane. It cannot be seen by the naked eye. If you are in a big city such as Los Angeles you can see the brown dirt that envelopes it looking like a dirty run down mess. This is smog and no one pays any mind to it. They freely breathe in those deadly particles every second and strangely do it without concern. You cannot see it unless you climb up to the top of the Hollywood Hills and look down on it or you are on an airplane landing at Los Angeles Airport. This tar is far worse than that as it is made up of dangerous energy.

You are all made up of energy. When someone gets angry around you, then everyone in that vicinity soaks that up ruining everyone else's day. It can incite unnecessary anger or sadness out of them. People are not accustomed to function on top of one another, as the energy is too intense and not conducive on Earth.

People are having Children that they should not be having. They make many explanations such as God has asked them to multiply. This was not what God intended. Man has taken it upon himself to decide what he expects are best for him and his surroundings allowing his Ego to dictate. This includes those that pick and choose from your holy books on what you want to believe in and follow. Most of the time they pick and choose the content that they believe gives them an excuse to cause destruction, wars, pollution or any other manipulative energy and harm. They use it as an excuse to suppress others and as a reason to justify their criticisms as if they are high and mighty and the rest have no business with life. This was not what God intended. He is wondering why all of the content on love and compassion – the most important parts of your holy books have been ignored.

Those that do not have babies for the sake of multiplying have had them out of ignorance, in poverty or to satisfy the Ego such as the hole and void within you. Others have children to save their marriage, relationships or to prevent their partner from leaving them. The only ones that suffer the most are the children followed by society.

There are some non-believers of God who contribute to the mass hysteria by allowing their Ego to give them free license to function as an animal might. They are irresponsible towards themselves and others by behaving without consequence. Who are you more likely to believe? Someone headed towards a path of love or hate? Those who choose not to believe do so in order to have an excuse to treat others or themselves unkindly. Now Earth is overloaded and crowded with toxins that are magnified beyond your comprehension. You are in a critical state that needs immediate attention and change within all of you. It is up to you as an individual soul to enact his change. No one else can or will do it for you.

There are those that have been called out into the open to usher people down the path of the Spirit. They are here to improve this world and fill it with the love and peace that God intended it to be. They are around you now or are souls prepping to be born into new human bodies for Earth's future. They are easy to recognize as some of them are ushering in peace while others are spreading love. They are working to clean up the environment and the surroundings on Earth. Some of them are teaching tolerance and love. You can easily recognize them as they have purposes that all lead to the same target: love, peace or joy.

You feel a euphoric happiness of joy when you are in love, experiencing love or giving love. You do not feel this when someone is seeking to harm, hurt or hate. These are the three "H's". You label each other with derogatory words. Most of them come from those that are rigid in their Earthly beliefs and who are blocked from love. These are construed as values when it comes to your political beliefs. This is a waste of time as what is destined to happen is already set. Inciting anger and hostility towards others will not sway it. Some will be happy with the outcome while others will be forced to adapt or fall more into anger and hostility. In the end no one wins.

The Devil sees you as disposable as he is what you have become. Your lack of love and help for your fellow man or your fellow brother has humiliated yourself. I am God. You are to love with all the compassion in your heart that I have given you from the moment your soul came to be.

One of your greatest challenges is that God gave you all Egos. There is no way to run from what might feel like a prison, but in essence is instilled to help you grow. Even the nicest most spiritual being has an Ego. This was God's plan since you are all here to learn lessons. You cannot learn specific lessons if everything is made easy for you. The decisions you make everyday make up your character. Your Ego tests you as the Devil would since they are one in the same.

Here's a scenario: You are broke and living check to check, but one day you find that your bank made an error and deposited $75,000 into your account. Do you notify the bank of the error or do you assume it was for you to spend it and you do? This is where someone's Ego can get in the way. It's where most of you were taught the differences between right and wrong. Be kind and accepting of your neighbor. How many of you are living like this? How many of you are teaching your kids this? In the example of the bank error, your decisions will eventually catch up with you and so will the bank and your authorities. Now you have committed an Earthly crime. You had not done anything like that before. This split decision happened when your Ego jumped in the way and dictated a false move on your part.

Because you are all born with Egos it is God's will for you to rein it in and keep it under control. The most spiritually evolved uses the least amount of Ego. Where you hear judgment from others, then this is the Ego at its worst. The Ego is the reason you have witnessed the destruction of God's planet. You were meant to take care of His gift and not destroy it. It is the reason there is abuse, violence, wars, anger, murders, ugliness and negativity. You have had centuries to improve and yet although progress has been made, boy, are you slow! It should not have taken you thousands of years to get nowhere. Why have so many human souls not caught up with the program? The energy of the world is a loaded gun and a ticking time bomb.

There are angels that alternate surrounding the Earth with angel wings covering the entire atmosphere to keep the energy contained 24/7. Earth is the most volatile, violent and hostile planet in the galaxy where everyone is firing harsh energy bullets at once. The Earth's atmosphere is like a pressure cooker that can destroy the entire planet. The energy emanating off the angels wings looks like stardust particles in a massive meteor shower. Only the sensitive, intuitive are able to sense it or even see it. They are the ones that are on Earth saving you from emanating destruction. The others including the abuse of power and yes even the self-righteous that are delusional into thinking they are good, are contributing to the damage. This includes those hiding behind false collars preaching erroneous, harmful information. Those that fall into Ego and attack back are no different. Peaceful interaction or no interaction at all from both sides is insisted upon in Heaven.

I am one in millions who serve humanity and Heaven to contribute to the improvement of a place to prevent it from rapidly dying. We gave you things like the Internet and cell phones to be able to connect and communicate positively with one another and look what you have done with it. It has grown to be devices for narcissism and cruelty. Thank God there are those who use it for good. The media and gossip channels are the worst offenders using the devices to lure in the most fragile who succumb to operating from the lower self full time. There is something we find eerie about strangers pasting their thoughts about what other people are doing which is perversely sick. This does nothing to improve your soul.

You have made Hell on Earth and it is what man creates for himself and others like him. The sooner everybody accepts this truth the quicker there will be peace on Earth. It is time for those who are on the receiving end of this nonsense to put their foot down and say, *"I am not going to take responsibility for you, because you are not doing your job. Your heart is closed. I will no longer be punished because of your indifference. I will not take responsibility because you have chosen to be unhappy and are thrusting that upon others."*

After centuries of evolution not only have you forgot how to love and spread joy to others, especially strangers, you have been stuck praying and hoping that one man, a President or ruler, will pull you out of your difficult and struggling lives. The difficulty and struggle you experience is your Ego.

Religion and Politics are two belief systems you have created through Free Will that cause wars, anger and hostility towards other human souls. Two belief systems that become completely obsolete and irrelevant the second your soul leaves your body. You are in the midst of grand chaos and it is time to wake up and snap out of it. It is more efficient and effective to have compassion and accept everybody's differences rather than trying to force them to change. There is peace and harmony that way and you accomplish more.

Everyone is struggling and suffering and they believe that someone in your government can fix that. It does not matter who is running things. You have all had the same issue decade after decade. After September 11, 2001 you saw the economy collapse as you went to war, then jobs were lost and businesses closed. Many of you lost a lot of money. Human souls passed away into the next life over the stress of being unable to find a job or due to the loss of their homes and families. You are arguing over triviality, over who should be allowed to marry who, and who should be killed and hurt. Where is the love? What happened to helping those in need? What happened to healing your neighbor and saying one kind word to someone else? Why are you not mobilizing to improve those living in poverty, the children or your economy and way of life? Why have you allowed your concerns to be misguided?

Politics, religion, bullies and your gossip media are the biggest and loudest Ego offenders in the world causing the most damage to the Earth. The damage that is done to other people is because they are operating from their lower selves. If everyone operated from there higher selves there would be peace on Earth. Everyone would be experiencing joy and love. We in Heaven see your flawlessness and your inner light. We know your most intimate intentions, thoughts and feelings. You can never get away with a lie in Heaven the way you can with each other on Earth. If on the outside you put on the act with someone to manipulate and get what you want from them, Heaven knows your true intentions and will block you in the end. You may briefly obtain what you wanted out of manipulation, but ultimately it will backfire, as we do not have your back if you have intention to harm, hurt or hate. We will never truly abandon you as we see the love deep inside you and will continue to guide you down the right path. We do not condone evil or assist those that seek to inflict pain or hurt on someone else. We want to work with each of you to improve God's Earthly paradise.

You are here to learn lessons and some of you have to go through it the harder way as you are newly here as a soul. Others have reincarnated repeatedly to gain spiritual wisdom while the rest have come into this life to help change and fix God's world. If you are cut off from spiritual wisdom and in being good to your neighbor and instead opt to do bad things, then you will have to repeat and repay that Karmic debt.

Crises mode was hit as you entered into the year 2000's. Your economy started to tank, jobs were lost, companies were closing up and then an abundant amount of your homes fell into financial ruin. This did not happen immediately so the average human soul might not have noticed. It happened in trickles until the energy around the globe grew to be particularly nasty. Adding to that, you have more people living on Earth than ever before. This magnetizes the energy that is put out there if you are operating from your Ego. You are granted Free Will to set up life as you see fit.

Around the mid-1940's having babies and lots of them became the thing that human souls decided was best to do. You call this the Baby Boom or the Baby Boomer age, which reportedly ran until the mid-1960's, but it actually continued into the 1970's and 1980's as well. It was what was expected of you by each other. You would grow up, become an adult, then immediately get married and start a family. You were programmed Stepford Wives. Looking back on history, you can see how and where you have been conditioned and programmed as a whole.

The world is now the most crowded it has ever been and people are suffering in all ways because of this. With the decline in available jobs many people around the world have been out of work. You have a rise in population and a decrease in available jobs. You have a rise in the cost of living for an apartment or house while minimum wage and the average job pay stays relatively the same. This is one of many imbalances in your lives.

The population will gradually decline over the years, as the newer generations of human souls are thankfully not looking to get married and start having babies. They are thinking for themselves as opposed to the bulk of previous generations. They are being born into new parents in order to stop this madness you have created. You may not notice this shift immediately. By the time the shift is noticeable it will take about another hundred years. It will be a more peaceful and accepting world then. We are moving out of your final Dark Age. Earth will one day be a place of massive joy that the upcoming generations are being born to will make happen. You are evolving, finding joy and are teaching it to many of your children and so forth now. It is a gorgeous mighty movement uprising in the midst of this negative energy from others. You are all each other's brothers and sisters. Encourage everybody to act and behave responsibly with yourselves and with those around you. This includes not having children you cannot afford or never wanted. You put it in your minds that you are under the impression that this is what God intended. He intends for you to love and to give love to everyone around you. Bring forth children only out of love and out of loving households and relationships.

It can be taxing to you soaking up all that nonsense energy out there in the world child. Walk away from those that express coldness or hostility towards you. You were meant to melt all of their icy hearts. Coldness in someone is a learned trait from when you were children. Coldness in someone is due to someone who does not or has not received much love or is ignored. This started with ones parents or society being aloof and dismissive towards that person during their critical developmental years. Coldness is not to be confused with introversion which is a shy social veneer that might make one seem cold, but is not once you delve deeper. Cold people lack love in their life and therefore need your assistance more than ever to see the light and joy around them.

One of your quests on learning to love is that you are tested repeatedly by those that may not be walking the talk or who are not spiritual, but superficial. While you are working on your life purpose and contributing to humanity and your surroundings in a positive way, you may wonder what they are offering besides annoyance and grief. God, Heaven and the Angels see the love and true self in every one of you including the worst parts of you. Your criticisms and judgments are wasted words and energy.

You have to share this world with those that may operate purely from the lower self. Some of those people are to have an Earth life and will likely reincarnate and have to go through it again if they do not learn something or grow on the first round. You are all evolving at different stages in your lives. Circumstances that might seem as if they are happening to you are actually happening for you in order for you to change and grow. This is a form of evolving. Otherwise you spend your whole life staying at the same level and not learning anything - which for some souls will do just that. They are unaware of the need to learn from the challenges and signs that life is giving them and therefore repeat the same patterns throughout this lifetime and future ones staying exactly where they are.

The generations have changed throughout the previous Dark ages. More and more parents today have come into this world at this time in order to incorporate these methods and spiritual principles when raising their children so that you will be that much closer to world peace and having harmonious and joyful lives. This is a far cry from the more rigid fear based ways of the past where certain customs had to be upheld and were passed on from generation to generation.

New crops of warriors of God's light are being born into this world to usher in this brighter shift of human souls by teaching about love and passing it down the family lines. It is a mighty movement that is being created. Those that are not on board are gradually dissolving out of the way.

FROM THE AUTHOR

The angry, negative or bitter way of living does not work anymore and nor does a lynch mob society. It's all just noise whenever people's Ego and values are bruised. People want freedom to say and speak whatever they choose only if it jives with their morals. It's the Ego and lower self that is screaming to be noticed and heard. When you experience worry, fear or unease over anything you are giving it energy and attention, both of which expand into more of the same. You do not want to conjure up a self-fulfilling prophecy and cause negative circumstances to hit you.

Do you ever notice that when something goes wrong, that it is followed by more of the same?

You may say, "Why does everything keep

happening to me?"

It's because you are planting heavy focus on it. Sometimes it's difficult at first to not feel distress over a negative issue, but it is important to take a step back and detach from it. The Ego can be powerful if you allow it to. It gets a rush out of controlling you and creating apprehension or fear about things that are not based in reality.

There is one way you can tell the difference between heavenly guidance and your lower self or Ego. When you receive messages from heavenly spirits, you will never experience fear, anxiety or dread. The messages they relay are full of love, even if they are warning you of something negative. There is still a sense of peace or an uplifting feeling that all is okay.

Chapter Two

WHAT HAPPENS TO YOUR SPIRIT AND SOUL WHEN YOU DIE?

There are varying theories and beliefs as to what happens when we die. I will explain what my Spirit team has shared with me over the years. They say there is no pain when you die. If there was a car wreck or someone was shot, your soul is pulled out of your body before that happens. Some of you worry that your loved one suffered death horribly with a gunshot or car wreck for example. My Guides and Angels have shared with me that there is nothing to fear or worry about as their soul exited the body beforehand. Our souls are designed that way. It is still possible for the body to be moving or jolting moments after the soul has left the body. It appears as if they are still alive, but they are not. They are alive in the sense that your soul does not die, but lives on. However, the body is no longer being used.

When your soul exits your body you may hear a sound or a pressure change when it happens. When we pass on, our spirit and soul goes into what appears to be a large tube or a gigantic tunnel that leads to a Light. I found this process into the different soul planes ironically similar to our own human birth that we are accustomed to knowing. The tunnel is nothing to be afraid of and in fact they have shared with me that you will have never felt this incredible. You realize that all the burdens of the body and the physical world had previously felt like one huge painful weight beforehand. You grow to become ecstatically happy in feeling the enormous joy you were born with. What you are doing and where you are heading as you travel to the other side feels perfectly natural to you.

The Light up ahead at the end of the tunnel grows brighter as you approach it. You are moving towards a paradise as one might have imagined it in their dreams of how Heaven or the Other Side to be. It is ten times more stunning than in your dreams.

Depending on who you believed in while living in your Earthly body, whether it be Buddha or Moses, that would be who would be in the mix of souls to greet you. If you were a Jesus follower, then you would immediately meet Jesus who welcomes you with open arms. If you were an atheist and you head towards the light you will be greeted by angels, your guides and past relatives and family from centuries back embracing you with a big party.

There is no judgment before God, but there is what is referred to as a life review. You go through a process where the bad things you have done are replayed for you. The reason is so that you own up to what you have done if you had not made amends during your Earthly life. This is not a form of torture and you are not being judged. The only judgment that is happening is your own as you feel, sense and know the brevity of how you behaved and towards whom. If you caused harm or hurt to someone, then that would be made known to you. Yes, even your ex-lovers will know what you went through when they hurt you. They will feel what you had felt with great veracity. The pain someone else felt that you caused is felt by you in a much stronger way than you would feel it as a human soul. Part of the reason for this is that as a human soul you have attributes of denial and indifference. This is shed as you exit the body.

When you were in your body and in the Earth's intense atmosphere you had a larger Ego than you do as you enter the spirit world. You have a much clearer mind and you are aware and affected by damage you had done to others on Earth. You know, see, feel and hear what you have done with great impact. You proceed from that point when you experience remorse and own up to your mistakes. This is part of your spiritual growth to move on to the next step. You have to make amends for what you have done or how you have caused pain to others. You will feel both how you felt as well as how the other person did in result of your actions. When you reach a place of forgiveness for yourself and others, then you move onto the next stage. You are shown the good things you have done and the impact that created as well. This is why it is important to examine your life now. Look at how you made it from point A to point B. You are going to have to do it when you cross over, you may as well get a head start. You do not have to publish a book, but you can write a timeline for yourself in a journal. I had at first wondered if people wanted to display their life story, but we do it anyway on social networking, reality TV and gossip sites, don't we?

There are different spiritual stages on the spiritual plane so you will not necessarily be in the same stage as other people are. This is the same as it is on Earth where everyone is at a different spiritual stage. We see this in all the religions that exist such as Christianity, Hinduism, Muslim and Jewish etc. The only difference is everyone on Earth is in varying spiritual stages all together whereas in the spiritual plane you are around those who are in similar stages of development.

If you were walking the path of love you won't be around someone like Adolf Hitler who has had to go through his own life review sessions when he crossed over. His sessions had gone on indefinitely as he was made to feel and experience the pain he caused in others just as we will do. Because he destroyed so many human souls, he is walked through each and every one of those souls feeling and experiencing what they went through. This is a lot of people he has had to go through and make amends with.

Hitler also took his own life, which has its own repercussions. When you take your own life, you are doing this before your time. There are several things that happen. Many who take their own lives have to go through another kind of spiritual training to get them to a place where they can assist those on Earth who are suicidal. There are some who may opt to go back to Earth and incarnate again for another run or class while others are asked to go back. If you exit before your time then you will have to repeat it.

Some of us are on Earth to have an Earthly existence, where others such as myself, were given an accelerated crash course of several lifetimes rolled into one for a purpose. They don't tell you what your mission or purpose is because you may rush to complete it before your time. Since I am someone who wants to get the job done immediately, they know I would no doubt get started right away. It is up to you to come to that realization on your own time.

When our souls exit our bodies, we are ushered into the Light, but you are not forced into the Light. If you as a departing Spirit are afraid of the Light due to fears of being told of Hell, damnation and judgment when living, then you may choose to avoid the Light. Atheists may avoid the Light or not truly understand what has happened to them. They might choose to stay in the Earth's spirit atmosphere, which is no place for any departed soul. That spirit stays stuck in what some might call purgatory or limbo mode roaming the Earth and attaching themselves to human souls.

If the spirit was a drug addict or alcoholic they will glob onto a human soul who is on Earth abusing or using those vices. They make it worse for that human soul by doing this as they coax that person on to continue drinking, doing drugs or any other harmful habits. These are the same spirits where people have reported Hauntings or a negative presence. If you are experiencing a haunting or a negative spirit, call on God and Archangel Michael and his band of mercy angels to take that soul into the Light. They can do so on your behalf even if the soul had previously chosen to avoid the Light. We have the power to request their removal on our behalf. I equate it to making a *citizen's arrest*, except they are not going to a place that is similar to jail, but going to a place they will later wish they had done so to begin with.

Many atheists immediately discover there is life after death and they love how they feel when they cross over that they do not doubt going into the Light as the process is happening. They remember who they were before they were born into a human body. Choosing atheism is a learned trait and a decision based on Free Will choice just as any other Earthly belief system.

The Light is nothing to fear, as it is all love where your wildest dreams can be conquered and felt. You can build that dream home you always wanted. You do not need money to buy it. Your Earthly burdens such as jobs and health worries are no more. You are who you were before you agreed to be born into an Earthly body. You experience God's love in ways you wish you had allowed yourself to be part of all of this Earthly life.

All the solutions you had wondered about while on Earth are answered. You come to the realization that it was all about pure love. You weep with tears of joy to know and understand that love in ways you had always wished you had. You discover that all of the things you took for granted were things as simple as the trees, flowers, the oceans, nature's wonders and above all love. You see how man is destroying the habitat and you wish you had done something to contribute to its survival. You can choose any route you like whether that is to train as a Spirit Guide, prepare the new souls that are arriving, or even reincarnate and have another Earthly life at a later time. There are many different paths and choices you can make with your team on the other side.

You may choose to reincarnate at just the right time in history to contribute something that will continue to improve the Earthly life. Earth life progresses slower than any other habitat. We are the slowest to learn and grow as a whole. When you cross over it is your inner light that is attractive and not your exterior looks. The brighter your light is, the hotter you are!

Many grieved in the year 2012 when a man shot his Mother multiple times and then went to a Connecticut Elementary School with a high-powered rifle to shoot many children, some adults and then himself. It was added to history as a perfect example of true evil that exists in human beings. The children's souls that crossed over were extricated from their bodies before the bullets hit. The day this happened when many were grieving and upset, I was shown that the children were doing great and were in recovery. This is not the recovery we think of after a surgery. It looks to me like a peaceful comforting and healing hyper-sleep. The souls were fine and surrounded by God's Light. Many angels nursed their souls to full potential. When the souls woke up they felt immeasurable love and joy. They feel no pain or grief during this process, but the departed souls are concerned when they see their loved ones on Earth upset. The children's souls soon visited with their grieving families not long afterwards.

Days after the deaths, my guides had shown the children to me at one of the most stunning gorgeous playgrounds one has seen in Heaven. They were surrounded by Mother Mary, Jesus and Archangel Gabriel – all of who are so powerful and unlimited they can be with anyone who asks. I found it interesting that they were the three that came through, because according to some religious beliefs, it was Archangel Gabriel who announced the coming of the birth of Christ and the new age of Pisces. Here Archangel Gabriel was with Jesus and Mother Mary surrounding the children's souls with their light after their passing.

Some have asked that if there is a God then how can He have allowed this shooting to happen. We are granted Free Will choice. This is in order for us to learn the difference between right and wrong as well as for our spiritual growth. No one in the Spirit world can intervene without your consent. The shooter's mind was wrecked with anger and pain from being bullied at the school beforehand.

The shooter's guardian spirits did attempt to help and stop him, but if you are not listening or paying attention to the communication that your Guides and Angels are making, then little can be done at that point. His mind had blocked out the Divine communication that was coming in with the wasted feelings of anger and pain. I was told that they did warn him as well as the mother repeatedly for some time, but both ignored the messages coming from Heaven as so many human souls do. This is why it is crucial for all of you to have a clear mind and live a healthy life so that you can pay attention to the Divine messages that are given to you to make your life easier. This is also why if everyone listened to their own Guides and Angels we would have peace on Earth.

When we cross over, our families from many of our previous lives, as well as our Guardian Angel and Spirit Guide, greet us in the spiritual plane. We meet our Spirit team and the ones we were communing with all through our life on Earth. You will know immediately that you are truly home showered with God's impenetrable Light of love. This

Light of love is so powerful that it may become so overwhelming you feel like you are going to explode.

You will know who the people are who greet you in the Spirit world even if you did not know of them while on Earth. Your memory of who you once were as a soul before entering a human body grows to be fully in tact. We meet our Twin Flame if they are on the other side waiting for us.

People often ask me if they can have sex or eat when they cross over. The answer is yes. All of our senses are awakened when we cross over and we are in peak form. If one wants to partake in certain pleasures they enjoyed on Earth they most certainly can. What they do tell me is there is a difference between that and someone who is obsessed by carnal desires. Satisfying carnal desires stops your spiritual growth because you are feeding the Ego and/or emptiness within you. This is not to be confused with having a healthy sexual appetite that is kept under control.

If you are reuniting with your soul mate or twin flame on the other side and you both had an active sex life or love together on Earth and want one in the spiritual realm, you may choose to continue. Only this time it is better than any other sex you have ever had because all of your senses are heightened to a great degree. You are not burdened with the physical problems that plague our human bodies and psyches such as daily stress, depression or impotence. If you have those issues while on Earth, they are lifted and left with your body when your soul leaves its human vessel.

I have had others ask me if the spirit world watches us have sex on Earth. The answer is no. They see us all as varying lights and have no interest in spying on you during fornication, unless it is harmful to your Spirit in some way. They are around to guide us down the right path and steer us away from danger or mistakes. They know your thoughts and feelings as well as what is to come for you in your life next if you continue on the path you are on. There are things we need to learn first before we reach a place of knowing our mission. For some people they may have known immediately what their mission was as a child, but might not have known how it would apply to them until later in life.

When you cross over you will be brought to peak form. This means any health issues you were having are no more. If your human body had gained tons of weight you slim right back down. If you used a wheelchair you would not need it when you cross over. Any deterioration you might have had happened to your body is rejuvenated. Although you can appear to others however you choose which includes the image and age you were when passing on. You do typically appear around the ages of 27-34 in human years. If a loved one on Earth has heightened clairvoyance able to see Spirits on the other side, you may not be entirely recognizable to them immediately. The reason is if you were overweight at that age or had a different look, you do not exude that look. It will look like you, but slightly different and more beautifully profound and strong.

We are souls temporarily inhabiting the bodies that we came into this Earth life with and then the body will be of no more use. The body is allowing us life on Earth to learn how to love and experience life lessons so that our soul can grow and be ready for the next plateau. In order to be on Earth our soul has to inhabit a physical body. The body is formed within a female human being whom you chose to enter this life from. Even if the woman gives their child up for adoption, you still chose that particular person to enter this life from knowing that she would not raise you.

If you live a long life, then the bodies you use will grow old as an indicator that your life run has been complete. Actual Earth age years have no relevance to anything beyond that. This certainly contradicts the Media and society's ageism discrimination that they have created and taught the public. This is a product designed by the Ego and is not based in reality.

CLAIRGUSTANCE

There was a night where I jolted awake to the smell of an exotic flavored sandwich. It was so potent as if someone was cooking it in my bed. This is a form of what some call *clairgustance* or *clear tasting*. This means that person can taste something that is coming from the spirit world. This sandwich I was smelling and tasting was coming from a spirit on the other side hanging around me temporarily at that time.

When this spirit lived an Earthly life in the early 1900's, he loved ordering these sandwiches everyday at his local deli for lunch. My light is so bright that these spirits are drawn to it. The light grows even brighter at night due to the fact that I am in a more relaxed state and away from the stress of the busy streets. I naturally inquired as to why he was eating when I was under the impression that you don't need food on the other side. One of my guides said, *"Your soul does not require food here. You are able to manifest the things you want or once loved when you were living on Earth."* This is true pending it is not harmful to your soul. In this case, this spirit wanted to continue eating those sandwiches he so enjoyed when living an Earthly life. Of course the sandwich is ten times better than the deli made it where he is now. The windows were closed and it was in the middle of the night. There was no one cooking and even if they were those smells never reach my room.

ABORTION

I have been asked about Heaven's views on abortion. There are souls in Heaven who want to have an Earthly life for the purposes of growth, learning or for a specific purpose that will benefit humanity in a positive way.

Those souls choose the people that will become their parents beforehand. I naturally had a difficult time accepting that I chose my parents, but it was for the objective of immediate soul growth. Sometimes before the souls have come into an Earthly life, they may play a hand at getting the two specific people to come together in love and marriage or at least to consummate so that they can be born into an Earthly life. They know beforehand which way it is going to go.

This same case applies to a woman who chooses to have a baby or wants one. If that woman goes to a sperm donor, the same process applies where that soul is choosing to be brought up by that mother. If the mother is a surrogate, the soul is fully aware that they will enter this life through that mother, but someone else will be their parent. They will know who that is as well, but will not have memory of this once born. If a woman decides that she wants, chooses or needs to have an abortion, then she is essentially preventing the soul from having an Earthly life. Someone responded to my statement, "So then you're pro-life?" I am not either. I do not make the choices for an individual and nor do I pass any judgment on either side. I merely relay what I am told and you take and do what you will with it.

The mother that is having this abortion is not technically killing the child as the soul experiences no pain. For the soul, it is more like, "Okay, back to the drawing board." The mother that is making the Free Will choice to have the abortion is in a sense preventing that soul from having a chosen Earth life. However, the soul that is aborted will have priority dibs on choosing another set of parents to enter this life with or they can choose to stay in the Spirit world and perform other functions and duties.

If a woman has a miscarriage then the same scenario still applies as well as if it were an abortion. If the mother who had a miscarriage or aborted a previous pregnancy is pregnant again, then that same soul is allowed to be first in line to re-enter the Earthly plane through that chosen mother. For those that have miscarried and eventually had a baby this can be comforting news to know that it is likely the same soul from before. The soul may choose not to re-enter, but may choose to be the Spirit Guide or Guardian Angel of the next child the mother has. Or they may assist the mother with not miscarrying at a later date. Exercise safe sex practices and be responsible when creating a baby.

Chapter Three

THE SOUL, SPIRIT AND POWER OF THE LIGHT

God is magnificent beyond human comprehension. His Light is vast spreading like a gigantic blanket that fills up every atom and cell that exists in any spiritual plane. He is everywhere including in every soul. There is no escape from Him. Archangels, Saints, Spirit Guides and Angels know everything about you from your thoughts and feelings to what is coming up ahead for you. Many of them can be everywhere at once. Imagine what God is like if He is even more powerfully prophetic than any other creation in the Universe?

God created everything in the Universe and all of the parallel Universes. Everything exists because of Him. This is why some say that you are born in the likeness of His image. They are not far off because you branched off out of Him. There are sparks of Light that shoot out of His presence. It looks like the kind of white sparklers that you might see in a firework, but there is an abundant amount of them shooting out. These sparklers are the individual souls that are born out of God. You came from Him. You formed out of Him. This is why you are born with the greatest qualities of God. Those qualities consist of 100% pure unconditional love, joy and a perfect state of peace. You are born into a human body in this state. Unfortunately, human egos tamper with this, creating a wide array of issues that wreak havoc on your existence in this life.

God would never hurt a soul. They are his Children after all. He would never ask you to hurt another soul in any way. You do have to develop your soul. This is why some of the souls he has created have to go to school. This school or class if you will is being born into a human body on Earth. Human souls are on Earth in human form for a variety of reasons. One of them is to learn lessons to develop and grow their individual souls. Other souls may be born in human form to teach everyone else about love or other important Godly ways. There are also souls born into human form who take care of God's planet in some way. This is part of how some souls contribute positively in the name of God. He expects everyone to display His best qualities, which are what you already have within you. This includes love, joy, peace and compassion. This is what a high vibrational state of being is.

He gave you an Ego that expands once you are in a human body in the Earth's dense atmosphere. The reason for this is in a sense much like a test. You are not taking the kinds of tests you would take in school, but you have other kinds of tests to take. These are tests where you learn lessons that enhance and grow your soul so that you can be your most magnificent self. When your soul enhances and grows, then your light grows big, bright and more powerful.

The brightest lights in human souls are those people who display high vibration traits. They are also the Children around the world. This is until those Children develop negative traits learned from their peers and adults, as they grow older. This dims their souls light. The human body you are occupying will reach a point where it will expire. This is no secret as everyone is accustomed to and hip with the reality that everyone will die at some point. There is no real death and end. It is only the beginning.

Your soul exits the body it was born into and the light of your soul expands as it crosses over to what some call the other side. This is also when your soul increases to perfection. You remember the lessons you learned in your Earthly life and you are brighter because of it. It is important to note that your ego will still be in tact. What this means is that if you were a nag on Earth, then you will carry this trait as you cross over. The reality of where you cross over to begins as you work on diminishing the traits you once adopted on Earth. This is why working on all parts of you now is essential. Where you head to after this life has no purpose for any of the nasty habits that you might have adopted while living an Earthly life. Nasty habits are what your ego is collecting at this time as if it has some value. It is corrupt and destructive. It aligns itself with what someone might refer to as the Devil. Your ego is the real monster and Devil at play here.

Take care of this planet and everything God created in it. Say enough to the volatile destruction of your surroundings. This cripples and harms other human souls merely to feed your ego, which has no worth or power in the end. It is time to wake up and take your life seriously. Humanity as a whole has become a spoiled, greedy movement and its time to rise above this weak ego driven mentality. This, 'kill or be killed', notion that there is not enough to go around or that you are better than someone else will die when you leave your current body. When in doubt always revert back to love and to express love.

*Saint Nathaniel's message
interpreted by the author:*

When you are done with your lessons and have fulfilled your life purpose, you will get to go back home. When you understand that reality, you learn that not only does none of this matter, but that you cannot take anything or anyone you've crossed paths with for granted. They all play a very important part in the process of your soul's growth. Not this body you're consuming. You are only inhabiting that space to move around in what might seem to some like an intricate design. Look at the false reality that this is not real in the way you identify your life to be. As a collective, you have advanced only in the sense that you have made this Earthly life place home. It is not home. It is school. Then you get to go home and talk about what you were lucky enough to learn while on Earth. What your Spirit team on the other side will ask you is, how about love? Did you remember to do that? Did you mend and forgive the Karmic relationships you intended to do? Or will you need to wait again for another long period of time before you both agree to meet up in a future Earth life to complete the cycle.

You created some wonderful things to function with one another. The lower self of your human mind takes advantage of it and treated it with disrespect. This is done in the same manner a child would when it is newly in human form. It reacts to things innocently and sometimes stomping out of turn naively. This child grows up to exude that same personality trait acting the way it did in lifetimes past. God is waiting for you to break the cycle that your soul continues to go through one life after another.

There are other similar realities to the Earth reality running in another parallel universe. We know this might sound like science fiction. Science fiction is what you have put in your entertainment to keep you busy while you function on Earth. This science fiction is not fiction at all, but stems from what some of you have seen in your mind's eye. World's different from yours and yet you discredit that this can be true. You're psychic beyond comprehension and even though human ego takes over and diminishes those telecommunication receptors with us, every now and then you still receive what you would call a hit of clairvoyance. What you're really doing is communicating with us. We communicate with you so that you can remember who you are and know what is important. We made this challenging for you, but so many of you are strengthening your soul and indeed have opened up to the other realities that exist beyond the soul lesson one you are having now. We watch the many souls growing and teaching others about us. Ignoring those who express doubt and remembering that you are not truly home. You will be home soon. Remember Him. When you remember Him, he can guide you down the right path to improve your soul. He will ease the burdens you experience and the turmoil and grief you often have. Bathe in His love for the kind of strength that wipes those negative emotions away. What troubles you is not real. All is well, we always say, to remind you that there is no reason to suffer when you are living in the light. The light protects you from the evil you sometimes describe.

There are different levels and branches of your souls. There are advanced souls in human form sent to teach you various things. All of the different things they teach lead to the same goal, which is love. Love is the thought form that began when God consummated. His love is overpowering since He is in every molecule, atom and cell. You cannot escape him. You cannot lie or cheat. You cannot deny Him. He is undeniable. He knows what you were thinking of yesterday and where you will be tomorrow. He knows when you will head back home. He knows what you will be doing before that time. He knows what you agreed with Him to do while living an Earth life. He knows when you have strayed from your path. When it is continuous and he sees you have given up, then He pulls your soul out of the body and you arrive back at home in Heaven. You know in that instant what you neglected to do while living in an Earthly life. You wish you had this epiphany when you were on Earth and amazed at how effortlessly it comes to you in Heaven. When you are Earth living in your body, connecting with us helps you stay on course and on path so that you do not stray too far from your goal. This goal is where the true happiness you are looking for lives.

There are ten dimensions from what I've been shown. They said that the first seven dimensions are various stages of where human souls are. Most move into the fourth after this. The higher the number of the dimension the closer to God is (even though God is everywhere), but He/She IS even more powerful and present in the higher dimensions. The dimensions eight through ten are filled with legions of Archangels, Saints or Ascended Masters.

Chapter Four

SCHOOL FOR HUMAN SOULS AND THE HELL DIMENSION

I have received numerous questions asking for additional information on things like why God would create human souls to begin with. Why create lights that are destructive and hateful to one another. The following is what God, Saint Nathaniel and his team of disciples have passed onto me at this time.

*Saint Nathaniel's message
interpreted by the author:*

God knows that all souls are highly spiritual. They just do not remember being in this state. He knows who you truly are as a soul before you entered an Earthly life. He

44

sees your soul as pure innocence and love. He understands that because He gave you free will choice and wiped your memory clean when you were born into a human life, that you will do and say things that are not of God. You must learn to grow and evolve even if it takes many lifetimes.

He knows humankind acts out of fear and naivety. You do not understand the concept of what and who you are in truth. You are led by your surroundings and human soul upbringing. You have to reach spiritual evolvement by branching out into independence and figuring it out for yourself. Some will have an awakening when they reach a certain age that helps them remember who they were before they were born. Others are too blocked and embedded in the material world. Therefore they stay blocked and stuck at the same status as when they were Children. They will have to repeat another lifetime and so forth until they come to the realization of what this is all about.

You are not less than you already are. Your ego has convinced you that you are. When your soul came into a human life, you were perfect in everyway. You became less than when you allowed your ego full control. You moved into this state when you allowed your material world to influence your actions. This stunts your soul's growth. None of the gadgets and material items that have been created to entertain you have any validity beyond keeping you entranced and pre-occupied in a timewaster. This delays your soul's growth and purpose. It is okay to enjoy yourself pending that it is not in addictive ways that stop you from moving forward.

God created souls out of his Light. What human nature understands as human, is a temporary vessel you inhabit for the sake of an Earthly life experience full of lessons and growth. An Earthly life is the bottom of the barrel, as you would call it. It is the lowest level as far as spiritual advancement goes in all of the spirit dimensions. It was designed for brand new souls to go to "school" in order to learn and gain knowledge.

God sends highly evolved souls to Earth as teachers, healers and leaders of various degrees in order to teach and inspire chosen souls that you might see as stunted in their soul's growth. These evolved or evolving souls agreed to come into an Earthly life for this purpose. The human souls who are stunted, is because they have allowed their ego to run the show and influence them badly.

You witness negativity, darkness and violence and ask why God would waste his time. His creation is not destroying themselves, because that is impossible. Your soul is eternal. The harm these particular souls cause are only harmful in ways that is understood on the physical Earth plane. He gave you free will so that you can learn what is right from wrong. The Earthly life is one made of students, new souls who are much like children that act out, and teachers who enlighten and empower in some way. There are vast reasons placed on each individual as to why they are having an Earthly life.

This is similar to the way humankind has

created schools around the world to educate you on the ways of human life. Unfortunately, they do not include spiritual or godly studies. They do not include the one reason humankind exists in the first place. You are allowed to set up life as you see fit in order to feel comfortable, safe and secure. These are humankind needs, but not real soul needs. It is much like chasing a mirage for comfort when the comfort, safety and security craved lies within reach. It lives within each human soul, which is a part of God who supplies all of your needs. God allows humankind to act how they please. This includes using His name in vain, and to cause hate crimes, destruction and violence. This may seem harsh, but those that do act out cause individual bad Karma, which they will have to pay back. This might take them lifetime after lifetime until they figure out that their actions are harmful and not of God. God is all about love.

There is a dimension in existence where souls who are buried underneath masses amount of ego such as eternal hate, destruction, anger, and bitterness hang out in. It's a dense atmosphere similar to the dimension that Earth resides in. It is no place for any soul. These souls are not cast there, but their soul moves into that plane willingly. Those particular souls are attracted to false desires.

They are the souls who chose to suffer, chose to be self-sabotaging or self-destructive while living an Earthly life. They are the souls that hurt others while on the Earth plane, either through violence, hate and even causing love pain, such as abandoning a love mate for selfish needs and priorities.

The souls in this dimension in question have very little love in their hearts beyond what they expect in return from others. They have an insatiable need and desire for the toxic material comforts that they craved while living an Earthly life. That dimension is the least evolved above the Earth plane. They are recognizable on Earth as they are also the ones who display negative traits on a daily basis. They are consumed with greed and chase needs that have no love in it. They are the souls that murder, inflict destruction and do not see the error of their ways. They are the ones that are oblivious to their surroundings and out of touch with their own soul and spirit. They are callous, but do not think they are. They only have a desire to be filled up with unreal selfish needs. These are the ones that may latch onto a human soul for the sake of coaxing them onto drinking, doing drugs or causing harm to another soul. They are the ones that cause pain in others on any level, only this time the pain is mirrored back to them in this dimension.

The dimension is dark and dreary due to their makings. It is made up of false mirages that evaporate out of the sands when you draw near it. They are the lost souls relentlessly intending on shunning any form of light. Their confused soul craves a perpetual escape and freedom that is non-existing. They design situations that are toxic by feeding their soul rubbish.

Destined to be stuck in that dimension until they come to true consciousness. This is by stripping away the selfish tendencies, greed, self-destruction and excessive carnal pleasures. This is by exuding love in all directions. Only then can they truly move forward. This is a rare and difficult task as these are the same soul's that lived an Earthly life who refused such love when it was given. They do not change when they cross over. They resist the tunnel of light that would only free them of harsh circumstances and bathe them in love. When someone attempted to love them on Earth, they rejected that soul. They do the same in this dimension unable to be penetrated by the power of God's love.

God's love comes to them in many forms including the soul mates they encounter. When they enter a companionship with one soul in a love relationship, then this is the highest form of love lessons for them to experience. The love relationship is what teaches you to love and to compromise. It is what is intended to teach you to give as well as receive equally. The love relationship teaches you to strip away your materialistic needs and grandiose narcissism when you allow it. It helps you remember what is important. It is the love of another human soul. Your soul benefits greatly from this form of relationship. The reason it benefits more than any other is because you are joining forces with this person who is not like you, who may test you and bring out uncomfortable feelings that you must face in order to expand your consciousness.

When you reject or ignore these connections that are divinely orchestrated, then you balk at God. This carefree nature is ego driven to satisfy what you want, which has no room for love or soul advancement. These are the souls that head towards the lifeless dimension as they cross over. They carry chains that hold them captive unable to break free of the padlocks of steel that formed from there materialistic and selfish desires.

Learn about love while you are living an Earthly life now. Do not wait until your soul crosses over into the dimension that awaits you, causing an even bigger delusion of who you are. Give love. Express love. Remember love. Do not treat others unkindly. Do not act out selfishly or recklessly with abandon. Remember who you are in truth and as a soul. Strip yourself of the toxic cravings you have that only weigh your soul down. Think of others and how you can serve humanity. You are not living an Earthly life to wallow in despair and pity or to chase greed or cause harm. You are here for love and to expand your consciousness. Take action steps to improve your soul today.

PAINTING WITH GOD

God has explained to me that manifesting is much like painting. I had never felt so naïve when I heard this. It seemed so simple and uncomplicated. I was always pretty on it, but how had I not come to understand this before?

He basically said that you envision what you want in your mind's eye. You hold the paintbrush in your hand. You gaze upon the canvas and paint your desires on this surface. There will be parts of the canvas that have yet to be painted. It will always be this way, since you are painting and erasing depending on how you are directing your thoughts. Your thoughts change, then without realizing it, you are painting over your previous image thus changing your reality in the process. You erase it and you paint something new. Sometimes you paint something bad and this is what you get. Sometimes you paint something good and then you back track. You think about what you want. When you do this you are picking up the paintbrush ready to paint this visual on your canvas, but then you take a few steps back. You stop yourself from painting the whole picture. You fear what would happen. You might actually like it.

I asked, "Is this why bad people that do horrible things sometimes end up succeeding?"

God said, "That is correct, my child."

Zadkiel connect me to God.

God replied, "I never left. You did."

How do I stay with you?

"You believe and it is done." He said.

He shows me an image of my soul on the other side as a Wise One and hunter. There is a bright light shining on vibrant flowers and the greenest grass. A radiant colored light shines out of my hands. Wherever I direct my hands, the light splashes images around me as if I am in my own painting. These images are the things my soul craves or desires. I asked God if this were possible.

He said, "You believe and then you doubt. This is how you disconnect from what you want. You forget who you are. You can create your reality. You do this where you came from before you took this current form. You did this effortlessly and never doubted. When you are home you will understand."

Are you one person or soul? Sometimes I have noticed that you refer to yourself as 'we'.

"I am everywhere. I am in your Guides. I am in the Archangels. I am in the angels. I am in every planet, every cell, every tree, every mountain, every human, every cloud, every particle, every atom, every centimeter. I am in the best of your self. I am in you. I am you."

I get it. Can you tell me more about this painting concept?

"I've already shown you. You read it back to yourself ten minutes ago."

I have the painting, but I was never painting the entire canvas. I would paint it, but then erase some of it especially the good simply by doubting."

"Now you understand. See the life you want and you shall have it. Never waver from this thought. If you negate that thought of what you want, if you are indecisive about it, then that is what you will get. Nothing. When you doubt that you will get what you want for one second, then you forget who you are and therefore receive nothing. As you are a part of me, you have the power to paint what you want and receive it. There is no class you need to take. You are the example. You are the Light. You are a powerful manifester. Paint what you want on this canvas. Never sway from the good you desire. When you sway, you forget who you are and where you came from. Paint the entire canvas. Keep it painted everyday or it will evaporate off the page."

Chapter Five

PRAYERS, AFFIRMATIONS, MANIFESTING

We are in a critical state as a human race. Many people are unhappy with where they are at in their lives reaching for a miracle or an answered prayer. You wake up in the morning and your mind immediately goes into worry or something negative. You know how this makes you feel and it's not pleasant. This is how you have set the tone and theme for your day. I have certainly had those moments in my past. Every morning my eyes open I move into a channel and communicate with my Spirit team. I may ask them, "Is there anything I need to know right now?" and/or "Is there anything you would like to discuss?" I will also let them know where I am grateful and thankful followed by positive affirmations.

Positive affirmations have a higher frequency vibration when you say them.

When you say this line: *"I'm broke and never have any money."*

How does that feel to you? It feels yucky doesn't it? I felt that just writing it. Well, guess what you're summoning? You're bringing in more of that broke stuff to you. How about instead you say something like: *"I have plenty of money. I am taken care of and my needs are met in all ways."*

Notice how saying that makes you feel.

Your lower self, which is the imposter self, will chime in at about this moment. *"Yeah, well I don't have a lot of money. I wish."* Or, *"I'll never get that job. I'm too old. I'm too fat. They want someone younger and better looking."*

When your Ego and lower self get in there, they seek to undo the greatness that you were born with. Your lower self does not want to see you happy or succeed. Your higher self knows there is plenty to go around and makes sure you are taken care of.

"I'm never going to get that job."

This feels as if there is a heavy weight of an elephant sitting on you. You suddenly feel low and worthless and begin attracting that same energy in. What spirals in is a domino effect of more things that only increase those feelings of low self worth.

Now firmly say believing it, *"I WILL get that job."*

Much better.

Now say, *"I HAVE this job and all is wonderful."*

Even better!

Say it as if you have it and mean it. Even if you don't have it yet, say it as if you do every single day and never stop saying it. This is what a positive affirmation is.

The three main aspects in our lives where people struggle the most are career, love and health. These are the areas that people often want to look at when they get a psychic or angel read. When you fight needlessly against the current, then your circumstances only get worse. This is due to the energy you are putting out there.

Because our souls often feel trapped in human form in this heavy and dense atmosphere, our lower self and Ego rises and becomes attracted to material and superficial things. Our souls are limited in our bodies for a reason, but the angels, guides and spirit souls are unlimited. We lose ourselves in outside events forgetting who and what we are.

If you use negative affirmations, then through the law of attraction you bring more of that negativity to you. You are always manifesting whether you like it or not so you may as well manifest what you want. Use positive affirmations and words when you speak, think or write so that you can attract that same energy in. Try it out for a week and observe how things improve for you. As you will discover, this will take practice, because it isn't long before the Ego gets angry and attempts to take over once again. It doesn't matter if your Ego fights you on it, because you can train your higher self to take it right back! Always revert to seeing things as working out positively in your life in amazing ways.

We have all at one time or another experienced a situation where perhaps our work life is on cloud nine, while another part of our lives suffer such as love and relationships. It may feel like one area of your life is mastered while the other areas are lacking in positive vibes. If you excel and shine with confidence whenever you are at work, then this is a good example where it comes to you naturally. This state is a positive form of manifesting. Your lower self does not question it or think about pulling you down. This is the same as creating a vision or dream board. You are saying the magic words without realizing it.

Look at how self assured you are at work. You can do it effortlessly and blissfully. This is the state where you manifest positive circumstances in other areas of your life. You have the positive visions in your head and know how to accomplish what you need to when you are at work. This is how I obtained the things I wanted in my life. I saw it in my mind beforehand, even though it would seem impossible to someone else. I didn't care. I knew and felt it in my gut and every cell of my body. I paid no mind to anything else including my lower self and I obtained what I envisioned.

Never discredit the power of prayer. I've spoken to people who do not believe in prayer as they do not believe in God or that there is a higher power. They may not pray because their prayers had never been answered before. They may suddenly call out to God when something detrimental happens to them or to someone close to them. God notices that we will often cry out for him suddenly in a panic. He wants you to always communicate with Him and not only when there is a dire circumstance begging for his intervention. He will of course intervene, but wishes to have a closer relationship with you beyond needing help.

Prayer has provided miracles over the centuries to millions of people. I have witnessed the marvels and wonders that have taken place by praying. It is not enough to just pray, but to keep an optimistic mindset. If you pray, but continue to fall into deeper despair, then pray for help with your emotional state. Once your emotional state is back to full power, then you are in that space where you can pray with detachment for the outcome of your desires.

Pray with intention. This is where you experience it everywhere such as your heart, stomach and mind. I have noticed great changes within and around me only after I prayed.

Prayers are also positive affirmations. It does not matter how you pray or whether you recite positive affirmations. It is all the same intention. God, the angels and your guides are right next to you hearing every word.

There is no wrong way to pray. Traditional religions have shown one often depicted as kneeling down by a bed with their hands clasped together while others may bow.

It does not matter how or where you do it. It can be done anywhere. You can communicate with God mentally in prayer as you are walking to your car, driving or sitting at a spotlight. Of course you won't have your eyes closed and hands clasped together in those cases. The point is that it does not matter how you are doing it. Just do it.

Prayers are communicating to God out loud, mentally or in writing. Prayers are asking for help or thanking God and your Spirit team for their assistance. Praying is praying for other people too! You do not want to be slacking in that department either. If someone is cruel to you, it is easy to want to lash out or become negatively affected. Try praying for that person who was cruel. Request that they receive intervention and assistance to operate from their higher self. It does not matter how or where you pray, but just that you do it. I would not continue with something if there were no results.

There are atheists who have protested that they do not believe in prayer. They may however sit with their own thoughts and ponder about their life at some point. They will feel grateful for what they have, what is to come or what they would like to have. Without realizing it they are praying. They are reciting or conducting positive affirmations and prayer. It is the same concept and intent regardless of what title you use to describe it. All of these thoughts, affirmations or prayers are heard and answered by God and your Spirit team depending on what it is.

There is often a bad rap from atheists also

with respect towards certain religions or people that pray to God. They may say something like, *"How can they talk to someone in the sky who does not exist?"* To them He does not exist, but to others He does. I do not blindly know that He, the Guides and Angels exist. I have experienced great circumstances firsthand by being connected to them. I have tested them by asking for specific things and would be privy to see it come true. I am always communicating with Him daily and subsequently receiving results.

It is important to remember that prayers are not always answered in the way you expect or hope. Sometimes they are answered in another way you never thought of. When it comes to God and Heaven, it is important to keep an open mind. Nothing has happened when I have not asked for it. I have mentally asked and then I watch it come true. Sometimes it is immediately and sometimes it is far off in the distance, but I never stop praying or believing. I know that there are certain things that are not happening, because there are certain pieces of the puzzle that have to come into place first.

Let's say that you are wondering why the right partner has not come into your life yet. It may be that you are ready, but perhaps your love partner is in a place where they are not ready to meet you yet. They may still be involved with someone that will not last. This is why you must keep an open mind and consider all the possibilities.

Always say thank you for being helped as well. Not just, "I need." The angels love it when you show gratitude and express thanks for what you do have. You do not want to become a spoiled child of God who takes and asks constantly. We are all blessed in many ways so take time out to say, "Thank you."

Every morning when I'm getting ready for the day I'm communicating with my Guides and Angels. There is not a day that goes by where I am not. Some of the things I do say to them are things like: *"Thank you for my health, thank you for the place I live in, etc."* I move down the list letting them know how grateful I am for the blessings that I do have. I feel more alive and alert when I start my sentences with, *"Thank you for...."* Those words have ferocious power.

Focus on being grateful and saying thank you for what you do have and watch how much lighter and happier you start to feel. You'll find that your life starts to be less tumultuous in the process. Being grateful and saying thank you raises your vibration to the level where positive manifestation occurs.

Your prayers will be answered in ways that benefit your higher self. You may need to get knocked around off your high horse a bit before you can see how your prayer is indeed being answered.

It can seem challenging to break out of a cycle of negative thoughts and words that so many of us use from time to time. It feels far easier for us to think and speak negative thoughts and worry. *"Oh I'll never get that job."* or *"No one will ever love me."* How about saying something positive? Oh forget about it! Choose not to live your life in misery. Choose to live happy and grateful. Choose not to allow your lower self to have control over you dominating your thoughts and mood.

You can pray for other people and send angels to intervene with someone else, but that person has to truly want help. The angels will definitely be by their side, give love, offer assistance and nudges, but if that person is not paying attention or wanting it then there is only so much that can be done. God and the angels will stay by that person's side continuously trying to get them to notice. They do not give up on you, but do you just give up?

Here are some examples of positive affirmations and high vibrational phrases:

"I am worthy."
"I have strong health."
"People like me."
"I have a wonderfully, successful career."
"I live in a beautiful house in the countryside."
"I have a loving and loyal partner."
"My opinion is just as valid as anyone else's."
"I am taken care of in all ways."

Don't short change yourself or be embarrassed as if you are not deserving of a great life. Heaven and your angels know you deserve it. They want you to be at peace so that you can fulfill your life purpose. You do not have to be on this planet to suffer.

Make a list with your own positive affirmations and recite it everyday either mentally or out loud. Do it before bed or when you wake up. Keep doing it until you have obtained your dreams. God, the angels and spirituality are like vitamins. You have to keep at it daily before you begin to notice the much needed improvement and changes in your life.

Not everything will happen right away. Sometimes for certain things there are life lessons that you must go through and be enlightened about on your own before the next step is shown. If you are feeling stuck at a dead end job and nothing is moving forward, then look at the lesson that is surrounding where you are at and acknowledge this. To do this you have to be completely unbiased and remove your Ego from the equation. Look at this dead end job in a positive light and ask yourself, *"What have I learned while I have been here?"* What positive trait did you gain while being there? This is your answer to absorb and learn from. Acknowledge it so that you are open and ready for your next step.

You can write your angels anything you want in a prayer. Tell them your fears and issues and circumstances you would like to change. Remember that when you pour your heart out to them with great purpose that you are truly heard. Then release it and move on with living life graciously and positively. Have patience with the outcome. Watch the miracles and changes happen in the coming months that follow as you continue with this positive mindset.

When you pray or recite positive affirmations always try to finish it with: *'This - or something better God."* Because they may have something greater than you imagined in mind and you don't want to limit yourself.

Your dreams and wishes come true, but sometimes not the way you requested. It will be in an even better way than you expected. It can be a major change or it can be subtle. Sometimes you will find you're still at the place you complained about, but then you realize that you're perfectly content there. They are keeping you somewhere for a reason and to fulfill a purpose such as getting along with a particular colleague. The delays can be that they have much to maneuver beforehand or have a grander plan that you cannot see yet.

Once again, remain optimistic and open minded to the outcome of your prayers. Know that there is a reason for everything that is happening for you in your life at any particular time. Know that you also have the power to change that simply by adjusting the way you think.

PRAYING FOR OTHERS

Praying for others has therapeutic effects. When you send positive words about someone else whether in the form of a prayer, affirmation or a statement, you are raising your soul's energy vibration. This process not only results in additional healing light sent to the other person, but this same light is magnified and re-directed back onto yourself as well. This only solidifies the theory that your thoughts do produce things, whether those thoughts are of yourself or someone else. When someone upsets you and you find yourself complaining about them, you are not only sending negative energy to that person, but that energy you're toying with acts as a mirror reflecting the same energy right back onto your soul. This is why it is important to catch yourself when you discover that you are spending more time using negative words about a situation and quickly modify them to be more optimistic. Sending prayers or positive words to someone else is a win-win situation because it not only has the added benefit of elevating the other person's soul, but it also improves yours.

Sending positive prayers and affirmations to others will help as much as the other person allows it to. They have free will choice to go against the prayers and override any heavenly assistance offered. If they are choosing to stay in a negative space or are making choices that their ego insists on, then there is little you or Heaven can do. The most they can do when you send prayers for another person is the angels will continue to uplift that persons thoughts and nudge them in the right direction continuously hoping that person will notice.

DISCOURAGED BY
UNANSWERED PRAYERS

Sometimes you pray for change with little to no instant results. When you notice that nothing has happened, your ego kicks in and causes you to worry. The ego wants things immediately. You start to lose faith when you notice nothing has changed. Your unanswered prayers sometimes have other factors that need to come into play first before you notice changes. There are times when your prayers are answered. The way it is answered might not be in the manner you expect it. You fail to notice the blessings that have indeed trickled into your life. There are the repeated signs you ignore that your Spirit team is asking you to do. It could be something as simple as signing up to take a particular class or go to a seminar. They put the signs in front of you. You continue to notice the same seminar flyer, but you never act on it or equate it to Divine orchestration.

Sometimes your Spirit team has to maneuver certain pieces of the puzzle before you notice the changes. Other times they want you to endure a particular experience as part of your karmic thread, life lessons and growth. The insight you gain in what appears to be a less than stellar situation carries over into your new situation. You have the revelation of why the experience was necessary. "Ah-ha, I see why it didn't happen right away." It all suddenly makes sense.

Recap:

Ask and you shall receive. Pray about the changes you'd like to see happen in your life. Have faith and believe in it. Focus only on what you desire to see happen and not what you don't want. "Please guide me to friendships with like minded interests, etc." Also add in, "Thanks."

Be grateful for what you do have. "Thank you for keeping me healthy in all ways. I'm grateful that I have shelter, etc."

Shifting your outlook can take practice and time, but before you know it, you will start noticing the positive changes happening in your life. Ask Archangel Michael to surround you with white light protecting you from lower energies when you pray.

A Prayer

"I'd like to thank God for creating this planet and its entire habitat, plants, wildlife, animals and the beauty of all of the nature surroundings. Help me to take care of it and never take it for granted. Thank you for providing me with all of the necessities I need to survive in a human body such as food, clothing, housing and money. Help me to align perfectly with my higher self and its purpose while here. Thank you for assisting me to express love always."

Chapter Six

JESUS CHRIST

Jesus Christ is one of the most powerful benevolent and compassionate beings in the Heavens that I felt compelled to mention him. It was important that I include him as he has been a huge significance in my life at times. I knew who Jesus was and had learned about him going to Bible School as a child. The images of him are everywhere around the world in Churches and people's homes. I have been privy to the negative words by those who claim to speak the word of Jesus. I have heard those same negative words coming from those who do not believe in him too. It can be rattling that one man can create such harmful thoughts in themselves and in others.

I had avoided him at all costs until he entered into my space during a spirit reading I did for someone one day. Jesus moved into the room where I was with immense force. He flushed through me and awakened every pore and cell in my body. I felt lightheaded and was prompted to pause as my head fell over. When I adjusted to his energy I experienced an incredible feeling of love than I had ever felt before. I didn't want it to end. I knew him as if I knew a friend without question or suspicion. I discovered the person that I was reading for was praying to him daily for healing. Jesus was coming in to reassure her that he is hearing her prayers. He was working on healing her ravished heart.

You have all likely had a love crush on someone at one time or another. You know the feeling of that crush where it's a roller coaster ride of excitement and immeasurable happiness. Now magnify that feeling by a million and this will give you a good idea of the feeling Jesus Christ conveys when he is with you. He is a magnificent love light and you experience it all over and around you. The tears you form are tears of joy as he has the power to blast away any negative emotion or block just by sitting next to you. You feel a vast greatness of love that prompts you to be moved to tears. You are overcome with emotion as if all pain has been dissolved from your soul and body. The weight of your entire life is lifted off of you.

I learned two things about Jesus that I was previously unaware of. He is all about love and healing in a grand way that I never knew or understood. No one ever talks about that aspect of him and it bemuses me. What I have heard or noticed were statements condemning and disapproving of other people. I have never received that impression when I have connected with him. In fact, the Jesus that I know is someone other than how others have described him to be. I wonder if they know him at all.

Jesus is a powerful healer and can work with you to have trust and faith in the miracles working for you in your life. His healing is done with an overflowing feeling of love that you may become dizzy or lightheaded. It is as if you are soaring above the clouds with joy. His presence is intense and massive that it is impossible to forget. He leaves an indelible impression on your soul.

Jesus said that his messages have been mistranslated over the centuries. It reached a point where they have now been so poorly interpreted that it is no longer his message. His message of course is simple and on par with all of Heaven and that is *love*. His main goals are always revolving around love, compassion and healing. My Guides and Angels continue to tell me that this Earthly run is all about learning to love and express love. Jesus only emphasized this with me, as he is the King leading the pack.

Jesus Christ is profoundly psychic and was as a man on Earth. He was one of the biggest healers and prophetic teachers we have had in history when he was living as a human soul. Jesus was and is giving, compassionate, otherworldly and full of love.

There are good people in every group, but in my research and in the media, I've only been privy to the negative words that others vocally shout when it comes to Jesus. This is why so many get uncomfortable when I say the word *Jesus*, because of the negative connotations associated with the name. His name has been so inadequately portrayed in the media by both sides of the debate that I have no idea who they are talking about. I have found that others I have met shutter at his name. When I speak of him, I speak of him because I know him personally. I have met him and communed with him. He has the most astonishing presence as a spirit that ever graced the Universe and the Heavens together. I admire and adore him. His presence and power is indescribable.

There are religions that believe your soul will be trapped in your body when you are buried if you have not accepted Jesus Christ as your personal savior. There are people that believe that some of you will burn in hell and bonfire. None of this is true to what Heaven has shared with me over the years. According to God's law they are free to live and speak as they choose even if it is not true. No one has had any experiences to report back regarding this alleged damnation. Whereas there are many who communicate to the other side who have received and reported countless accurate information regarding a stranger's loved one. They relay information to that person about their loved one that is accurate and confirmed by the other party.

I have spent my entire life experiencing first hand of what the truth is by conducting my own communications with the other side. The helpful information being fed to me ends up coming true. This was how I grew up and there is no other belief system that can or will ever sway me. Discover the answers for yourself by doing the work and not living in fear.

Jesus wants you to work on being a good person always striving to improve yourself. He wants you to do the best you can to operate from a place of love. Anything less than that is unacceptable. I don't respond to any other source no matter what they claim. It has no bearing of truth to me and nor will it ever. I do not act purely on faith and trust which is why Heaven had to spend so much time in my life convincing me. When I started seeing and experiencing results, I knew that they and it were real.

We have heard stories from others that have said that Christ is coming or that they are the Coming of the Christ. Christ is not coming and nor is that person the coming of the Christ necessarily. Jesus Christ is one of the most powerful spirits in the Heavens now. He can be with every one of us at the same time if we ask him to. What I have been told by him and my Spirit team is that Christ is not coming because he is already here. Due to the fact that he can be with so many people at the same time, he is also living in many of us. He is unlimited in that pieces of his soul exist in certain people. These are the people who do the work of bringing others together, who teach about love, who teach about humanity and compassion. These are the people who live in this space and are doing his work because they are channeling him often unknowingly. He is not coming in the way others have guessed in creating a hole that swallows up mankind. He is already here in many of us doing HIS and God's work.

The coming of the Christ is already here and we are all around you. Some of you may not even be aware that you are doing his work, but you agreed on it before you arrived. Live as Jesus did. Love yourself and your neighbor. Work together in healing one another and this world today.

Whether you're a fan of Jesus or not, you cannot deny the impact he created. He is the reason Christmas is celebrated around the world. He is the reason some call the end of December, "the Holidays". I would love to meet the soul who has never heard of the word Christmas. His messages are about all love and all healing. He is not about anger or judgment. He is not about living your life in stress or greed. He is all about the uplifting joyous kind of love. This is why he was sent to Earth in human form. It was to teach that and spread that around. No one is going to listen to a spirit being. If they did, then we wouldn't have the drama that exists all around the world. This is why many souls come into the Earthly plane in human form to send reminders and do the work for the Light. There are millions of human souls who have wandered off their path and forgot how to love. They have grown to be indefinitely lost with no hope in sight.

Jesus is not typically the light I call in. He visits me to connect on rare occasions regardless. When he does, those are the moments where I feel the indescribable kind of love that doesn't seem to exist on Earth. It's an incredibly powerful euphoric feeling. You feel like you're soaring above the clouds.

Before I entered this Earthly plane in human form, Jesus was one of the final spirits to approach me before I came to be here. He said what I would retain from the spirit world would be love.

He whispered in my ear, "Remember all that matters is love. You will forget at some point. You will find your way back to that essence. When you do, you will remember who you are. *We* will immediately connect with you when you are born into a human body."

He said I would be tested in unimaginable ways in order to know what human suffering was like. Since on the other side I had no clue. I watched others on Earth suffer, but I felt nothing. I was detached. It was detachment with love and not a cold indifference. There are different levels in the way spirits feel and perceive things. As a warrior on the other side, I had some measure of disconnection. All I knew and understood was taking care of business. I've incorporated that into my purpose here.

GOD HAS A PLAN FOR ME

Some have used the phrase: "God has a plan for me." This is half true. Those who have used that phrase have forgot that it is YOUR plan too. You made the agreement with Him before your soul entered this life in. You know what His and your plan is. It is up to you to discover what that is. No one can tell you what it is. It was removed from your memory bank on purpose so that you can stumble on your way to discovering this plan. If you did not stumble, you would not grow and evolve. What matters is how you glide over life's challenges and become a stronger soul because of it.

There is a lot of selfishness, rebelliousness and ego in the air coming from those who are not seeing the real gifts that exist in their life. Count your blessings on a daily basis. The "poor me" or "I wish things were different", way of thinking will only make you feel more stuck. It blocks positive manifestation and you dig an even deeper hole into a bottomless abyss.

MOTHER TERESA

This huge burst of shining light wanted to live in the trenches on Earth in order to make a difference for this planet as a whole. She never wavered from her quest, which was solely focused on reaching out to the poor, the hungry and the destitute. Her light was so bright to begin with, that it gave them all hope. Tirelessly she forged on even when faced with doubts that God existed. As a human soul, she had at times forgotten where she came from. Visiting those that are ignored by the world, she witnessed the conditions they lived in and couldn't understand how God could abandon them and how He could not intervene and help them. She would only entertain this uncertainty once in awhile. When that happened, Jesus lifted her up each time she expressed reservations. This is understandable to feel like your fight is worthless. It may seem like you are at odds with the world, when you are really fulfilling your mission. Your own life is sometimes challenged in the process of your life purpose.

She crossed over and works as an Ascended Master on the other side once again. For those who tirelessly work on their life purpose in ways that help many people, or in charity, and who express doubts of God and wanting to stop, she visits you to lift those qualms off your body making you strong and whole again, so that you can forge on as a warrior of light. Known to human souls as Mother Teresa, she will strengthen you as she has come through for me from time to time. You can call on her to work with you when you feel like throwing in the towel and giving up on your quest. She radiates a light of love so magnificent it would astound you. Her work continues on the other side, as it always has, to help those in need. She does not fall into ego and instead adopts the mantra that all of Heaven lives in, pure love and joy.

When Mother Teresa, also known as Agnes, came into an Earthly life, she immediately got to work and did not waste any time absorbing herself with triviality. She was on a mission that would carry on her entire life and beyond.

What have you done lately? Don't forget who you are and why you are here.

Chapter Seven

WHAT DOES HEAVEN SAY ABOUT HOMOSEXUALITY?

It would be remiss of me to not reveal information on one of the most controversial topics that exist in present day. I did not intend to, but my Spirit team had urged me to considering that it is playing a big part in the darkness pervading the planet.

Someone who does not understand another or who hates another they don't know with immense venom is a product of the Ego and fear. There are many people who want to see death against homosexuals while others attack, condemn and harass them. There are those that hide behind the words of false prophets who claim to speak the word of God. I know the word of God and have been with Him long before I had this Earthly existence. No human soul is any more special than any other.

I discovered that the words *homosexual* and *gay* are not in Heaven's vocabulary and therefore nor are they in mine. I will put down as best I can what God, Saint Nathaniel and my team of guides have relayed to me on this.

Saint Nathaniel's message
interpreted by the author:

We attribute no labels to your souls in the way that you have trained yourself to. You choose this act on your own volition of Free Will. You are all created in the likeness of His image. Things such as judgment, maltreatment and murder are what is considered a sin in the eyes of God. Homosexuality is not a sin in the way you define it. We have to use words that you are accustomed to understanding.

The world is experiencing a transforming shift organized and set out by God. This shift is part of the evolution of His creation in order to bring it back to the grace and beauty intended from its inception. You are responsible for it and how you set up your own lives. The world is at a place where there is as much good as there are bad. Dark energy pervades half of this world dictated by human Ego. The other half is filled with the light of God. This is the dawn of the new age upon us. You witness this darkness in the constraints you have created such as politics, government, social media and those in power. These branches seek to interfere with others in how they live. They persist to obstruct how others choose to set up their Earthly life as a human soul.

The Light in you is growing in numbers. They are the newer Earthly souls electing to come into this Earth life to work in making significant changes to the planet and its habitat. They are what you consider the new generations of people. They are peaceful loving and in tune to their surroundings with limited Ego. They are more privy and conscious to how they and others behave with others. They are stripping away unnecessary toxic ways of living from addictions to poor behavior patterns including escapism.

Many organized religions are broadening their teachings. Others are using their placement to condemn and curse certain human souls who appear differently to them. Those souls elected to arrive in ways you do not understand in order to awaken your hearts so that you may grow spiritually. This is a way to accelerate the planet as a whole in reaching a place of love and compassion. Some of you may have a tantrum or want to stop what you are afraid of. You cannot stop what God has intended.

You have had same sex marriages centuries ago during what you call the medieval times long before you made it currently an issue. These same sex marriages stopped around the 340 AD period due to the rise of Christianity and the Christian Emperor's who passed laws forbidding it. They were infused with fear and instilled this same fear into the public. Because they did not understand the true nature, they called it a crime and punishable by their own new laws that they saw fit. This was all man and Ego created, not God created or inspired. Eventually the punishment was to be burned alive in public. This is still happening in third world countries. They have carried out with hangings as if it were 400 A.D. Some of these countries continue to stone them to death by bashing them in the head with bricks. They attribute this to the Devil. What they don't see is that the real Devil is how they choose to react. Your Ego makes excuses so that you can justify causing others grief and harm.

You are witnessing the destruction towards homosexuality being reversed hundreds of years later where you have progressed becoming more compassionate and loving towards one another. You are all of God's children and loved equally. Why do you not do this my child? Why do you fret and experience so much pain and anger so? What truly offends your fragile Ego that someone has another path that is not like yours? Do not lose sight of who you and your soul truly are and will become when you have completed your Earthly life.

You are not going to Hell for French kissing. You will not go to Hell if you are in a committed love relationship with someone of the same sex. There is no Hell in the way that you know it. The only Hell is the one you create for yourself. The shivers you feel are a product of living in fear and the unknown. Do not be afraid my child. The only fear that exists is the false reality your mind tricks you into believing. We understand you do not fully comprehend what Earth's existence is about. To hear this may seem like you have had the rug pulled out from underneath you. You are always safe and always will be.

Some of you are reacting in ways that have been taught and trained by other human Egos. You must stop what you are doing and the way you have been thinking to date. Eliminate all of the noise of the human Egos around you and focus on the stillness within you. When you truly let go of all the burdens you carry on your soul by others, will you then see the truth of who you are dear one. The obsession that some have over homosexuality or race and religion is diverting the world from love, joy and their life purpose. You have a preoccupation over a breed of God's creation that you do not understand. Your Ego allows this to cause uproar out of fear and misguidedness.

God, the angels and Heaven see no distinction between heterosexuality and homosexuality as long as two people, two souls are in a loving, committed relationship. We are always happy to see love being observed. Your souls are attracted to one another. Your genders are irrelevant and not based in your current reality. When you leave your body, your body does not come with you. Your soul is left in tact along with its Ego. You must realize this as part of your lesson and growth.

Some of you have allowed your Egos to feel uncomfortable with homosexuality. You have allowed it to control you into forming warped thoughts into your minds that it is perversion, pornography and sex. This exists regardless of the human souls attraction to one another. Two souls born of the same gender who experience similar love for one another, know God by this act. They are no different from any other soul who craves the love and companionship of another. They have elected to come into this life as a homosexual knowing that they will put up with tough lessons at the hands of newly developed souls. They know they will put up with it by those who have had their Ego guided by another.

You are all here to set up life and provide for yourself regardless of who you choose to do this with. Those that seek to condemn homosexuals often do not know others who are homosexual. The truth is that they do. Those who have an attraction to the same sex surround you. They are forced to hide their true identity for their safety or to avoid ridicule or punishment from their communities.

Many use the holy book as justification to revile others after having misread and abused the text to give them license to conduct harmful acts. God does not support a justification of evil, anger or hatred even if you have decided that your holy books do. You added text to your holy books at a later date to condemn Homosexuals. These were men with human egos who experienced living in limitations and were misguided by fear. It is a danger to use God as your reason for your harmful justifications as God only sees the innocence in your soul. These men had no knowledge of homosexual relationships. They feared homosexuality and anything that appeared to be different than what they were accustomed to in their communities. What they were accustomed to was self-taught by the society they lived in. It was not and is not God's word. God's word is simple dear one. Love. Learn to love all of His creation and you shall know God. If your Ego seeks to find ways to explain why you condemn, harm and judge others, then you do not know God or the Holy Spirit. You can only reach God by experiencing love, joy and peace. You can reach him by keeping your mind clear of the addictions and toxins you escape for. Do not act out aggressively towards another because they are different. This is a product of fear and not the love you were born with.

Men of the cloth and those of the like have chosen to set up and run organizations that support human laws where countries may place rules on their unholy books to harm others. These laws seek to put homosexuals behind bars and even death. They are perpetually foolish and disconnected from the Divine Creator. They are dictated by rules earlier souls of thousands of years ago claimed to be receiving from God. Yet, there was no more input from God afterwards? Did God stop communicating? He can never stop communicating child. It is you who have stopped listening.

You have men donning as preachers speaking for God that you publicly assassinate the homosexuals. You have been doing this act for centuries persecuting anything or anyone who was not like you. You have done this with the Indians, the African Americans, the Asians and all of God's races. You have done with this with others who do not practice the same religion you do. You have done this with all souls who are not like you. God did not create a world where everyone is the same. You must stop allowing your Ego to control you into experiencing fear and anger because you have met someone who is not like you.

Some of you will say that you love everybody. We wonder who would befriend one who disapproves of them. You misinterpret holy text. You pick and choose what suits you for your life today while ignoring the rest and giving no compelling reasons why. God knows your actions and what you are up to. You may deceive another human soul yet you cannot cheat God. You live erroneously and savagely as if you are doing right. You are not doing good when you condemn and harm one of God's own creations.

You have Free Will laws made by God where you may set up your life however you choose. We cannot intervene unless you specifically ask for our help. If you have come into your life as a homosexual you would do well to remember your divine heritage and pray for God to assist you in making this world better for you and those around you. This will speed up the process to peace on Earth.

Many homosexuals and new generations lack in faith or do not believe or buy there is a

God. This is understandable considering that growing up as a human soul all they have heard and read were stories of sermons from churches or their community calling them sinful and the Devil. You are not sinful. It is your unruly Ego that is the Devil. There is no sin when it comes to love and who you choose to love. The rules apply to you as much as they do with all human souls. Treat yourself and the people around you with compassion, kindness and love. Do not choose the role of a monster. We watch over you and guide you away from a state of mind that chooses suffering. When you feel empty you reach for harmful pleasures out of hoping to fulfill a void. We do not condemn how you choose to live. We hope and urge you to do right. We cannot cease to love you.

We do not support the need for you to have several partners whether homosexual or heterosexual. This need you desire acts to temporarily fill a hollowness within you that demands carnal pleasures of the material world you have created in order to escape from your unhappiness. You are seeking to fulfill an absence that you believe to be missing in you. This desolation that grows into loneliness is God's love you want. It is the only love that can fill you up whole and help you to remember your Divine soul heritage. It is your Ego that takes over convincing you of harm. There is a distinction between two people in a loving and committed relationship forging an alliance regardless of their human genders. The discrepancy is wide when compared to a relationship that chooses to have more than one partner. This speaks to your sensual urges that are satiated by the Ego.

There is a difference between a man who is in love with another man in a committed relationship and a man who is lying in bed with many different men. This same concept applies to a married or committed man or woman who lies in bed outside of his commitment with many others outside his home. There is a difference between being an upstanding hardworking soul and one who is not. We do not talk about one man and one woman. We speak to you about two souls who join together in your Earthly lifetime to express love and cherished commitment with one another.

There are millions of souls who agreed to come into this lifetime as a homosexual understanding the repercussions that will come about. There are some of you who say that you were born this way when this is not technically true. You might have chosen to come into this lifetime as a homosexual. Your attraction and feelings are not chosen. As difficult or incomprehensible as this may be for some of you, the truth will be revealed to you when you are ready. This is why it is imperative to do the learning and growth work now. You do not need to wait to do it when you cross over. There is no fire and brimstone expecting you. The only judgment that you face when you cross over is your own.

There are homosexuals who feel the entire world has turned against them. Imagine what happens when you believe that you are hated.

You are not hated in truth. Your Ego functions at full force when you crave attention and love seeking it out through destructive relationships, sex or any other toxic addictions. Be clear now and invite God and the Holy Spirit to fill your soul up with the love you require.

God knows what is to come on the planet. He has known the trajectory for centuries. He knows what His creation would do and how they would behave. He knew the souls he created were naïve and innocent in their anger and actions. He still loves you regardless and only wanting you to be at peace. He wants you to grow and learn. He does not want you carrying around these unnecessary and unhelpful burdens and emotions. You have allowed your material world you created to overpower and control you. This has weakened your communication with God. You can resurrect it and develop it back with focus, practice and study. When you do this you will discover the same truths of where you came from. You will discover how to improve your way of living. This requires a lifestyle change some may not welcome. This new existence will be more inviting than you have come to know.

You have been abused, you smoked, drank alcohol, did drugs, slept with more people than you can remember. You never found what you were looking for, did you child? You come face to face with misery and your self-esteem plummets further into a deep abyss. You used these manufactured outlets as ways for you to quiet the noise of your Ego.

They were ways to feel loved and wanted.

Release the need to continue abusing your soul. Allow your world to open in ways you have always dreamed of. The unnecessary outlets of escape harm your soul, your body and yourself. You desire the almighty's love. He will give it to you no matter who you are and at no cost.

FROM THE AUTHOR

To give you an example of the brevity of what young people are going through, a sixteen year old guy writes me: *"My whole family thinks liking guys is a disease. They make me sad."*

His family does not know any better. It's not a disease. Anger and lower feelings are a disease. Some human souls are on the lower end of being an evolved spirit. This is why those chosen ones were sent to Earth in human form first to learn something before they can graduate to a higher spiritual plane. If they do not get it right or learn anything while here, they will have to come back to Earth again repeatedly until they have mastered it.

You can't reason with someone who does not know any better and believes what they were taught by others. They have to figure it out for themselves or they will when they cross over. Often people are poorly influenced and advised growing up. They believe certain things are wrong without knowing anything about it.

A good Christian woman walks the talk and lives in His presence. She never judges and has a 'live and let live' attitude as long as no one is being harmed, but is exuding love. She lives in goodness. Another woman lives in His presence except she fumes with judgment and negativity. She does not live in His goodness, but the wrath of her own Ego.

Jesus absolutely does love and accept you as I've discovered through my connections with him. You have to be completely removed from both sides in order to connect to anyone in Heaven. You are not removed if your views are set. It is learned behavior or your Ego that has set these views. These same people crucified others into slavery. The same types of people are doing the same thing to homosexuals or those who are of a different race or culture.

Do not allow your Ego to control you into thinking that these people that use the Jesus name to attack you as being accurate. They are hiding behind his name and using him so they can have an excuse to misbehave. God accepts and loves all that He has created despite what some religions teach.

Whenever you do something good or bad this is filed away in your Akashic Records. Archangel Metatron holds these records and stands near the throne of God during your judgment. All of your Guides and Angels are highly developed psychic entities that know your probable futures, your map and life purpose. They keep you heading in the right direction. You must pay attention and communicate with them so that you stay on course and do not experience anger or sadness.

The Archangels are the managers of the angels with profound and powerful psychic perception. God's abilities are beyond what you can comprehend. He knows what's up ahead backwards and forwards. He knows what you are going to think before you think it. He knows how you will proceed even when he hopes you will choose wisely.

God saw the technological age that would bring everyone to connect more efficiently. You can now easily find out what someone in China is doing if you are in the United States. The Internet was created to bring people together, but it has magnified the anger and the noise. Human souls are flawed and has predictably abused what it is given. People follow each other and pat one another on the back when they are doing wrong. Human souls have such capacity for greatness, but they refuse to budge. It is not God or Heaven that takes issue. It is sections of society that take issue. They are afraid to embrace all people, unless all people live as they do.

When you do not understand something it is important to take the time to understand it before you can draw a conclusion. It is important to walk in your fellow man's footsteps and understand what its like to live in their shoes. I do not subscribe to traditional religions that promote low self-esteem, fear and guilt. I do believe in the power of prayer.

Growing up I continued going to Church

because I enjoyed it into my teenage years. I felt secure and safe by these people who were seemingly good hearted. I was not at any Church that was screaming fiery hate words, but they were speaking of love. The reason I stopped going was because I received all I needed to. I already knew the real truth about all of us because of my communication with Spirit. I was ready to move to the next level rather quickly. I continued moving through each level as they kept my class lessons and growth accelerated. This does not mean I had it easy, but far from it.

This is a world that shakes its fist in anger, "Hang him!" This is without knowing if there is guilt or not. Even if there is guilt, it is not our place to pass down judgment or punishment. Mistakes are made in this lifetime to be corrected. Nothing has changed from the days of hanging witches that were not witches, hanging someone because of the color of their skin, feeding Christians to the Lion's because they had different belief systems, assaulting homosexuals because they love someone of the same sex. Human souls have much to learn and have still not grasped their purpose here, which is as Heaven has said: Love. You are asked to live with and be with those that are not like you to build up your tolerance to learn to love.

The highest reported rates of hate crimes in America are racially or anti-gay motivated, but there are some officials who do not report every crime as anti-gay motivated even when it is. We live in a country and world where there are crimes acted out on another human being because of where they are from or whom they fall in love with. These are people who have to suffer because someone doesn't understand it or is uncomfortable with it. Identify the real lower self in that passage. All of the souls on this Earth are here to share it amongst one another regardless of your interests. No one owns this planet, as it is God's creation and world.

My Guides and Angels have all told me that Same Sex Marriage will one day be open and legal throughout not just the United States, but the entire world eventually. They would not tell me when, only that is in the future. They added that it would not be anything that bothers anybody. No one thinks twice about it. God allowed us to set up shop here as we see fit even if we are instilling rules that are incorrect. It is not how our souls entered this life to begin with, but was rather molded by the communities and influences others had on our souls growing up. The main reason we are all here and have agreed to be was for the purpose of love, which I will hammer down until the end of time. All of the rest of the nonsense is "the noise" as they call it.

Chapter Eight

LOVE BIG AND LOVE ALWAYS

Human souls often choose to live in fear and obsess over power and control. In this state they infuse their lower self into the Holy print in the name of God. They paint false pictures to control others through guilt and fear. This is what they consider to be a moral way to live at any given time in history. The only ethical range that exists is your own character. You are here to make your own choices and decisions as to the best course of action for yourself. When you make a poor decision you pay for that consequence. Every time you get knocked down you are experiencing a lesson. Each lesson you learn helps you to grow to be a smarter and stronger soul.

God and the angels will never stop loving you. It only pains them to watch you suffer needlessly. They see no need for you to exude anger and other wasted emotions and feelings that have no positive power over anything in the end. Those feelings are reactions that your Ego objects to. The only true power that exists and overcomes is God's LOVE.

Keeping our Ego quiet is up there on one of the most difficult tasks for us to do. We're human after all and born with these Egos that we wrestle with daily. We have these Egos in order for us to learn necessary lessons that assist our soul in growing and evolving.

How many times are you going to allow yourself to get knocked around before you wake up?

When are you going to grow up and be fully aware of your actions, your thoughts and how you treat others?

When are you going to learn right from wrong?

When are you going to learn to love unconditionally?

When are you going to learn to treat others with respect?

The best way to quiet your Ego is by stating positive affirmations that all is as it should be and everything is taken care of for you. Even if you do not see your desired outcome yet, you need to act and believe as if it is already here. You need to live in a state of gratitude and feel joy for this life you have been given the opportunity to have. Do not let someone else's Ego stop you from your purpose and goals.

When you look back on your accomplishments you may have noticed that they came to you when you were not struggling for it. It came to you naturally and effortlessly. We all want things immediately. There are reasons that your desires are delayed or are not instantaneous. Some of the common suggestions the angels urge us to have are patience, trust, faith and love. Try living in this state every second if you can. Practice it regularly and do this especially when you know you are being tested like when you get a flat tire and you're late for work.

Do you ever notice that when you push for a relationship to happen with someone that it ends up back firing and not going as planned? This is because you cannot push for anything including love.

As far as love and relationships go, those that merge blissfully are when both of you are patient allowing it to evolve on its own course.

In order to improve your life the first thing you will need to do is reduce or eliminate your addictions, bad habits and even some friendships! When you ask your heavenly spiritual guides for assistance you may be prompted to make crucial life changes that you may not feel ready to make. They have you do this because you are being prepped for something greater up ahead. Before that can happen, you will have to strip away all of your toxic baggage. You may be absorbed in it to the point that you might not be aware that it is poisonous. They do not ask you to do this because they are against the fun you have when you have an alcoholic drink. They do it so that you can live a more blissful life full of happiness, success and love. They know that vice is only a temporary high that is not long lasting and delays you from moving forward. You're too busy battling the side effects from your addiction to have enough energy to focus on what's important. When you continue on with your former toxic way of living this gets in your own way of success and holds you back. You may remain stuck at a dead end job you do not want to be at. When you have all that poor energy around you it blocks good things from entering your life.

This is about stripping down to your soul core and eliminating particular behavior patterns and lifestyle choices that are disruptive to your soul's enhancement. It can take some time dissolving these things, as the changes do not happen immediately. They will be met with some resistance or unhappiness. You are shredding all of the bark around the tree that is part of your life experiences, so that your true inner light of God shines as bright as the sun. Once this is done then you will be shown your next move. This can be digging up those projects, ideas and anything you have always wanted to do, but were stopped by procrastination or negative self talk. You will attract in friendships and relationships of a higher caliber on your new improved level. You will stand in your own power with great strength and there will be nothing that you cannot do. The flood gates open for you to tackle and accomplish your dreams. When you get started the universe will meet you tenfold!

At the time this was written and complete around the holidays, I connected with Mother

Mary and Jesus Christ for any messages to incorporate in here. The message they gave me was to experience joy now. I know for some of you that might seem like a difficult place to get to. There are things that you can do to elevate your feelings into a happier state of mind. Do something fun with a friend. Surround yourself with other people who lift your mood. Watch a comedy or a lighthearted, feel good movie. Blast some good music. Stay away from negative substances that will only bring your vibration down. These are things such as news headlines or going out to places when you know it's going to be packed tampering with your energy.

I am out there in the trenches with the crowd's everyday so I get it. I temporarily placed myself in a part of town that borders soulless on purpose. You could call it research or just plain crazy. I witness harsh energy regularly. I conduct frequent sessions of shielding every day because of this. I am careful with what places I head to, what time of day it is and who is around me.

The morning before Christmas Eve I witnessed many people rushing around frantically and unhappy. They were pushing and shoving each other aggressively. Some were even getting into fights that were taped on cell phones of onlookers and uploaded on You Tube. Others waited until the last minute to shop since their heart is not in it or they are functioning with no time and energy.

A friend of mine who was out there as well called me to ask, *"What's going on with everybody?"*

People have lost sight of what is important. They are hurrying around doing what they feel is expected. The only thing you should be doing is getting back into the joy of your life. Regardless of your spiritual beliefs, it is unavoidable to know that the Christmas word is meant to be a time of joy. It is the kind of joy you should be reaching for daily. You should be celebrating! You should be celebrating this life and each other.

Remember what is truly important to your soul and why you are here. It is to love, to give and to spread love. This mantra should be adopted everyday and every minute of your life. Deep down your soul knows what you can do to bring yourself back. Know your light. Know your power. Know what you were born here to be. Be one with the Light and one with Spirit. They are waiting to walk beside you, in front of you and with you. They see us all holding the hands of our neighbor no matter what they are into or what they are like. If you treat your neighbor without love, then you don't know God. When you see yourself and others with disgust, then you only know the Ego and the Devil.

Love is who I am. Love is the source of all that I wish. Love is the source of power. The more that I love, the safer I am. The more that I allow myself to love the more powerful I am. Sending God's light and love is not enough. It is powerful and necessary. Some of us have a soldier nature in the name of Heaven and we do have to fight. When I say fight I don't mean with violence, but by being assertive in our stance. We have to stand in our own individual power. Think and speak for ourselves even if we stand alone. All of our goals are to unite as many people as possible in peace, love and joy.

Have zero tolerance for anger, violence and hate, which gets everybody nowhere. Yet we cannot be a doormat either and nicey-nice all the time. There are some of us who are specifically here to exude the characteristics of love, which warms the coldest of hearts. We are an army of workers of the light who all have varying and specific gifts to contribute to ushering the world gracefully into a new age. This is why we elected to show up at this time in history. This is how we all found each other. It's all connected. We are all connected. We are soldiers and fighters of the light. We are warriors in the name of God and Heaven. I am a warrior of light and I exude the honor that God desires. Join me in teaching this message so that we can shift and change this world for the better, one person at a time.

Connecting with the Archangels

The Archangels are powerful, benevolent beings of God that are present to assist us along the right path. They are the managers of the angels and are non-denominational which means they do not belong to any religious establishment. It does not matter who you are or what your beliefs are. Like God, they are available to anyone who asks for their help. There are legions of Archangels residing in other dimensions. I will focus on sixteen of the more popular Archangels. Included in this you will discover what their roles and specialties are.

Several of the Archangels have been featured in the different holy books. Others have reported sightings or visions of an Archangel when they needed the help most. There have been religious followers who I have heard say that you are not supposed to worship Archangels or angels. No one is advocating that you worship or pray to the angels because all exaltation goes to God. The Archangels are gifts from God to help each of us experience love, joy and peace in our lives.

In order for one to hear and communicate with God you must be completely at peace. You must be feeling and exuding joy, love and compassion. You have to be living in your higher self. You need to be in this state and stripped of your ego.

God wants to communicate with us, but you do not hear God unless you are in that state of higher consciousness. This also means that those who condemn and harm others in the name of God are not communicating with God. They are instead operating from their lower self and ego. You cannot communicate with God in a state full of blocks.

The Archangels are God's gifts to us to help us reach that place where we are fully able to communicate with Him. The Archangels are his messengers who deliver God's messages and personal guidance to us. Everything the Archangels communicate are God's word. They raise our vibration so that we can indeed hear and communicate with God Himself. Although God is always communicating with us, we are not listening if we are experiencing negative feelings such as anger, stress, hate or even sadness and depression. This is why the Archangels and angels come in to lift those unnecessary emotions. They assist us in diminishing our negative ways of thinking.

The Archangels names end in *'el'*, which means "of God". The only two exceptions are Archangel Metatron and Archangel Sandalphon who are the only two Archangels who were once man in human form.

I am always communicating with some of

the Archangels everyday. I correspond with them everywhere. I may commune with them while I am in the shower, walking to my car, driving, riding in an elevator and the list goes on. I call each in as a reminder that I appreciate all that they do for me and others. Since they are God's arms, you are communicating with God too. He wants to have a relationship with us. He wants us to always communicate with Him. It does not matter where or how. It is not necessary to do it in a church, but it does help to do it in a calming environment. You can communicate with Him mentally while you are brushing your teeth, while you are driving or jogging. It does not matter how or where you do it, just talk to Him!

Calling upon God, any Archangel, Angel or Spirit Guide can be done at any time and anywhere. They are all powerful and unlimited which means that they can be with anyone and everyone simultaneously. The Archangels each have specialties that they can assist you with on your journey. They are magnificent Lights and like God, they know your thoughts, feelings and desires. They show up before you have finished your sentence! You do need to ask for them in order to help you since they cannot interfere with your free will. This is God's law. The only exception is if there is a life threatening moment taking place that may result in your premature death. They will appear in your life to put a stop to it. Many around the world have witnessed and professed stories of their encounters with the Archangels.

One of the more efficient ways of connecting to any Archangel or enlightened spirit is by creating a soothing atmosphere and environment. You can do this in a quiet room that contains soft music playing, a candle burning and the smell of incense. Breathe in deeply and exhale out any stresses or thoughts until you are fully relaxed. Call the Archangel by name and pour your thoughts and heart out to them. Do not push or attempt to receive any sort of communication otherwise you will block it. Simply just "BE". Remain open while allowing whatever messages or guidance is being communicated to you through any of your *clair* channels *(seeing, hearing, feeling and knowing)*. You do not need to create the perfect ambiance in order to communicate with them. However, you may find it will relax you and bring you to a blissful state where your connection is made. These spirits are highly responsive to the light of a candle and a calming environment.

There is no greater feeling of freedom than connecting with Spirit. You can do this anywhere, but in nature or peaceful locale is ideal. Only then do you experience the weight of your burdens and worries being lifted off your soul. You realize that nothing else matters. All of the restrictions that the human ego forces upon other human souls are not real. They are a product of the lower self, which is born out of fear. Learn about some of the specialties of the more popular Archangels in my book, *"Connecting with the Archangels."*

SPIRIT GUIDES AND ANGELS

$\mathcal{H}$ow often do you find yourself thinking about nothing in particular when suddenly a jolt of clear-cut information flies through your mind? What you receive is so commanding you experience a surge of uplifting joy coursing through all of the cells in your body. The idea, key or answer you gained was the missing piece of the puzzle to something you needed to know at that particular time.

How many times have you received a nudge to do something that would positively change your life? Instead of taking action on it, you deny it chalking it off to wishful thinking. You later discover that it was indeed an answered prayer if only you had taken notice and followed it.

These are some examples of how you can tell when it is your Spirit Guide or Guardian Angel communicating with you. When you get yourself and your Ego out of the way, then that is when the profound answer you had been hoping for is revealed to you. The impression you acquire is so powerful that it pulls you out of the darkness you were previously stuck in. It is a bright light shining its focus directly onto the message in unadorned view. It is crystal clear as if it had been there all along and you wonder why you had not noticed it before.

There are so many joyless faces out there waiting, complaining or praying for a miracle. What you are looking for is right in front of you and closer than you think when you have faith and believe. Instead you choose to fill your days up partaking in activities that only erode your self-esteem and overall well-being. These are things you are not even aware of like sitting in traffic completely tense. You experience another mundane routine day screaming for an escape from this prison of a life you have created. You stay unhappy in your jobs, the places you live in and with certain friendships or relationships. You ponder over not having that home of your dreams or sharing your life with someone in a loving relationship. The days having this dull mindset turn into months and years with no miracle in sight. This disappointment grows causing you to appear eternally glum, negative and bitter. Those emotional traits mask your disappointment and heartbreak attracting more of that to you.

To cope you drown those nasty emotions with addictions from drinking heavily, ingesting chemicals, doing drugs or by partaking in time wasting activities such as gossip and Internet surfing.

You choose to be disconnected living behind a wall built of your own attitude and yet it is in your basic human nature to want to connect to other human souls, to someone or something. You want to be happy, but that state can feel so out of reach and unobtainable you drown in its thoughts.

Our way of communicating today is primarily through phone, texting, email and social networking. Even if you truly wanted to sit face-to-face you are too busy or worn out to bother. You were not intended to live your life in misery and unhappiness. For some reason, you choose to fall into a pattern of suffering. We as a whole are to blame for this design.

It is never too late to improve your life. God, your angels, spirit guides and all in Heaven can and want to assist you out of this hopelessness. They are always there next to you wanting to lift you out of your life of desolation. It does not matter what your beliefs are and whether you are religious or an atheist. It does not matter what your race is, whether you are rich or poor, gay or straight, liberal or conservative. Whatever you agreed to come into this lifetime as, you are loved equally. No one is more special than anyone else.

God and the angels see each of your inner lights, your innocence and your true purpose for being here. If you have veered long off course, they can help you get back to where you need to be. Who you are is a perfect child of God and love no matter where you are from or who you are.

Available in paperback and kindle by Kevin Hunter,

"WARRIOR OF LIGHT: MESSAGES FROM MY GUIDES AND ANGELS"

There are legions of angels, spirit guides, and departed loved ones in heaven that watch and guide each of us on our journeys here on Earth. They are around to make our lives easier and less stressful. How many of us pay attention to the nudges, guidance, and messages that are being given to us? There are many who live lives full of negativity and stress while trying to make ends meet. This can shake your faith as it leads you down paths of addictions, unhealthy life choices, and negative relationship connections. Learn how you can recognize the guidance of your own Spirit team of guides and angels around you.

Author, Kevin Hunter, relays heavenly guided messages about getting humanity, the world, and yourself into shape. He passes on the guidance he was given by his own Spirit team on how to fine tune your body and raise your vibration. Doing this can help you gain hope and faith in your own life in order to start attracting in more good stuff.

𝒜lso available in paperback and kindle by

𝒦evin 𝒽unter,

"REACHING FOR THE WARRIOR WITHIN"

Reaching for the Warrior Within is the author's personal story recounting a volatile childhood. This led him to a path of addictions, anxiety and overindulgence in alcohol, drugs, cigarettes and destructive relationships. As a survival mechanism he split into many different selves. He credits turning his life around, not by therapy, but by simultaneously paying attention to the messages he has been receiving from his Spirit team in Heaven since birth. He explains how he was able to distinctly tell the difference between when his higher self was intervening and ruling the show, and when his lower self was running his life into the gutter.

Living several lifetimes in one, he did not let anything stop him from getting his life together, going after what he wanted and achieving it. He describes how he pulled himself up by his bootstraps and obtained every job he wanted without prior experience. This is from work in the entertainment industry with some of Hollywood's respected talent, to ridding himself of toxic addictions and living a healthier lifestyle clear-minded.

Kevin Hunter gains strength, healing and direction with the help of his own team of guides and angels. They navigate all of us through the treacherous waters in our lives. Living vicariously through this inspiring story will enable you to distinguish when you have been assisted on your own life path.

Reaching for the Warrior Within attests that anyone can change if they pay attention to their own inner guidance system and take action. This can be from being a victim of child abuse, or a drug and alcohol user, to going after the jobs and relationships you want. This powerful story is for those seeking motivation to change, alter and empower their life one day at a time.

The Warrior of Light series of books available in paperback and kindle by Kevin Hunter,

 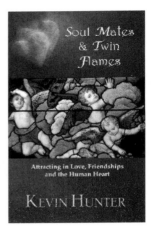

Spirit Guides and Angels: How I Communicate With Heaven

Soul Mates and Twin Flames: Attracting in Love, Friendships and the Human Heart

Connecting with the Archangels

Divine Messages for Humanity: Channeled Communication from the Other Side on Death, the Afterlife, the Ego, Prejudices, Prayer and the Power of Love

Raising Your Vibration: Fine Tune Your Body and Soul to Receive Messages from Heaven

About Kevin Hunter

Kevin Hunter is an author and love, dating relationship expert born with piercing insight into the human condition which he receives through clairaudience and claircognizance cues. His books tackle a variety of genres and tend to have a strong male protagonist. The messages and themes he weaves in his work  surround Spirit's own communications of love and respect which he channels and infuses into his writing and stories. His books include the Warrior of Light series of books called, *Spirit Guides and Angels, Soul Mates and Twin Flames, Divine Messages for Humanity, Raising Your Vibration, Connecting with the Archangels* and the greatest hits book from that series, *"Warrior of Light: Messages from my Guides and Angels"*. He is also the author of the self-help autobiographical and inspirational book, *"Reaching for the Warrior Within"*, the horror/drama, *"Paint the Silence"*, and the modern day erotic love story, *"Jagger's Revolution"*.

Before writing books and stories, Kevin started out in the entertainment business in 1996 becoming actress Michelle Pfeiffer's personal development dude for her boutique production company, Via Rosa Productions. She dissolved her company after several years and he made a move into coordinating film productions for the big studios on such films as *"One Fine Day"*, *"A Thousand Acres"*, *"The Deep End of the Ocean"*, *"Crazy in Alabama"*, *"Original Sin"*, *"The Perfect Storm"*, *"Harry Potter & the Sorcerer's Stone"*, *"Dr. Dolittle 2"* and *"Carolina"*. He considers himself a beach bum born and raised in Los Angeles, California.

Visit www.kevin-hunter.com

Made in the USA
Charleston, SC
09 February 2014